Disclaimer

In no way is this book based on any lore or historical practices to my knowledge. This book is meant to be for those who practice their own UPG (Univerified Personal Gnosis) or SPG (Shared Personal Gnosis). It is meant to show my personal work with the Norse gods and in no way to reflect how people of the past practiced their religion. I am not a reconstructionist. I am simply wishing to share my practice with others of like mind, who may be experiencing or interested in such matters concerning spirit working, or Seidr in some way. I understand that everyone's opinions will be different. Keep in mind while reading that this is all formed from UPG and SPG from myself and of others who may practice similar things. I consider myself to be a devout Hard Polytheist to Odin, as well as to other Norse gods and goddesses. The practices and mentions of such deities are specific to me and in no way do they reflect all persons in Norse Paganism.

Chapter 1

My story

When I was a teen, I began searching for something in life, something with meaning. There was a lot of disbelief, as well as skepticism involved in my original search for religion and spirituality. I never expected for things to end up the way they are now. I never expected that I was being followed or even watched by a deity. I didn't believe in those things, not back then. I had a very pantheist view, and my best understanding about the universe or religion in general, was that maybe gods could exist. Maybe that some how they were guardians or avatars to specific places on earth. Maybe they had many faces, or maybe they were all individuals. Most of my thoughts were assumptions, speculations in which blocked me from seeing things the way I do now.

I was dealing with a lot of personal issues. Then there was the odd and unusual experiences that dealt with shadows. Have you ever seen something out of the corner of your eye? Did you think it was just yourself? I had so many ideas about if I was really going crazy or if something strange was happening to me. I had a lot of experience with these forms of spirits. Spirits that had the intention of making me feel odd, or depressed. I would see them, sometimes physically, and other times mentally. I began to question my sanity for a while until things kind of moved on for me, and everything disappated into a completely devoid sense of spirituality and religion. I didn't know what to believe but I wanted to believe something.

Once I was free of my personal problems, I began researching religion and spirituality again. During this time, I had an unusual obsession with corvids. This obsession lasted for a long time, a few years at least. I had my screen names related to ravens, the clothes I wore, the wallpaper on my computer, etc. Everything was about ravens! I then got this idea in my head one day to start researching different gods and goddesses associated with magic. Magic was something I had always been interested in, so of course I wanted to find a deity associated with it! I was searching through names on wikipedia (I know, not the best resource!), and I ran across the name Odin. The more I read about him, the more I began to feel connected to him in a way I couldn't really describe. That's when I saw it, his association with ravens and how they were his messengers.

I began an intense research about Odin. I bought an Odin statue, and had it sitting there for reasons I couldn't really figure out. I got so into the stories that I had to learn more. I picked up a few religious books on the subject of heathenry, all relating to the term Asatru. The more I read, the more I liked it, and the more it resonated with me. I read about the popular lore associated with certain deities and the various history that involved the religion as a whole. Authors like Diana Paxon, Galina Krasskova, were my first books in starting out. They were very interesting to me. I then began my path to studying heathenry at that point. Other books followed, books by various

3

people like The Our Troth, Raven Kaldera's book series of Northern Tradition Shamanism, Teutonic Magic, and many other titles and authors.

Beginning with reading the first two authors I mentioned above, I wanted to start practicing something religious. I wanted to make this religion part of my life as well as a way of life. I adopted the Nine Noble virtues in a way where they helped me to remember what is important to me, but never in an extremest way to control others. I wanted to be a better person and to use them to help me better myself, but they were more like guidelines instead of rules. Since I had previously bought a bust statue of Odin, I began to setup my altar. I had various tools like a couldron, candles, a chalice of water, etc. After a time, I began to make my own candles that I felt were associated with specific deities. I felt connected to other Norse gods and goddesses. The first two goddesses I began to call to after Odin were Frigga and Skadhi. Skadhi helped me deal with some personal issues I was having, but we'll discuss that further on!

After about a year, maybe two had passed, I felt this urge to do more. I had read a lot about taking an oath to a deity and the dangers that were sometimes involved with it. I began to contemplate if I should do this, and if it was right for me. I felt no other place in life was calling to me, I had no skills to speak of at this point in time. After careful consideration, I had decided to blood oath myself to Odin. I did this for reasons that involved a friend. In return I would serve Odin as a god slave. (Yeah, I know what you're thinking and it probably involves insanity, but this is my story so, that's the way it happened for me.) I spent months and now years, doing various work and skills. All for the purpose of the blood oath I made to him. I began to feel and "see" things I hadn't been able to before. The more I meditated with him and gleaned from those meditations, the more my practice and devotion changed, the more it changed me.

There was a point in my life where I became to blunt, to straight forward. I had to adjust myself. Some people say that I come off very jagged, like I think I am the best. I can assure you, I have no desire to become popular, or think that I'm the greatest thing there is. It's actually quite the contrary. I didn't wish to offend people, so I had to work on my people skills. Sometimes when you work with deities, you start to mirror some of their traits as well, which is very off-putting.

I read more books and began to understand and see things in a way I hadn't before. I began to adopt the term Northern Tradition Pagan, or perhaps Norse Pagan or Heathen. I didn't adhere to the Asatru way of things. (Asatru means true to the Aesir. The Aesir in my terminology are gods and goddesses associated with Odin, Thor, Frigga, and many others of Asgard.) My studies involved spirit working as well as working and learning the runes. Many deities showed up after my initial workings with Odin, his wife, and Skadhi. Freyr, Freya, and Thor. They decided to approach me in meditation after a time. Thor especially, was very understanding with me! Then there was Loki, the god with the worst reputation you could imagine! We'll discuss my work with him later!

After a time, my work involved praying to them every day on a specific day of the week. I felt bound because of the oath I made, and I also felt as though Odin had tricked me into doing it some how. A lot of my practices involved just praying, meditation, and journeying. I would do breathing exercises in which was intended to break me free of my physical bonds so that I could fair forth into the spiritual. After that, I was expected to read cards or runes for people as a service. A few job requests were about spirit removal and healing. I would go to a persons house and remove a spiritual influence, which was usually some kind of black shadow that had attached themselves to a particular person. Healing started with online sessions with people in which I would spiritually journey to their place and perform a rite of healing. This later became a common practice with Eir, a goddess that is known for her skills in healing.

This brings us up to current time. My practices now are pretty much the same. I have taboos. I'm not supposed to cut the back of my hair, I'm supposed to accept all requests for readings unless I'm told not to, and the glorious job of my most hated service of all, God Mouthing. (Just typing that makes me cringe. It is essentially the one thing about my practice I absolutely hate for various reasons.) I know the lot of this is crazy, I know it sounds crazy to claim that someone could even be in direct communion with the gods, and I know how controversial it sounds. You don't have to tell me, because I already know. I already question what I do and if it's real. At the same time, I have learned to accept the fact that this is what I am meant to do. The bottom line is, this is my practice, my way of life. You don't have to agree with it, you can judge it all you like. It won't change anything or the oath I made. I don't view myself any better than anyone else out there. You are all equal to me. This is just my personal UPG and experience. Please take it as just that if nothing else!

Chapter 2

Spirit-Working

This is a very popular and very controversial subject. There are many beliefs associated with this type of work as well as many practices. I believe that everyone has a different relationship with the gods. I believe that just because you have a taboo not to cut your hair, doesn't mean other people have to abide by it. Taboos are specific to the people they are bound to for various reasons. Working with Gods is a form of spirit-working. What is spirit working? It's a form of practice associated with spirits such as ancestors, deities, and various other spirits like dwarves, elves, nature spirits, etc. It's a practice that revolves around working spiritually with spirits of various races and cultures.

While spirit-working is a very popular thing for a lot of different people, it's actually very dangerous. If you don't use proper spiritual protection or you're not protected by a deity, you can run into some serious issues. I knew a girl who once was bound to a very malicious spirit, who would bug her and torment her at night. She would have horrendous nightmares and actually feel physical pain at times, like something was pulling on her chest. I also had a friend who began their spirit working with a pendulum and some spirit came along, thought it was funny to pretend to be some other spirit or deity and say weird things. It would make the pendulum freak out, and scare her half to death by making the spirit board say crazy and frightful words.

I'm just going to recommend to you right now: Don't under any circumstances get involved with spirit working unless you have a firm grounding in your belief system. You need to understand how to protect yourself. It's very important to have a basis in protection magic. You can save yourself a lot of trouble by researching things first before rushing in head first into things you don't understand.

Spirits are not here for our entertainment. They exist like we do, and sometimes if you get involved with the wrong ones, you'll find yourself in a horrible situation. Many spirits, like the shadow spirits that I have mentioned before, can be very parasitic. They can cause a lot of mental problems, including things that match to depression or bipolar disorder. Sometimes they can just encounter you. Possibly you dabbled and they stuck themselves to you. (Just because you're depressed however doesn't mean you're under spirit influence, you should always check to see if you have any form of mental disorder before assuming you're under spiritual attack!)

Before I started working with spirits, I had a firm understanding of magic and the theories behind it. I also had the protection of seven deities before everything started coming into play with them. While most of my work deals with otherworldly gods from various Norse worlds, I also have other spirits whom I work with occasionally.

Working with Green Wights

My first encounters with any form of nature wight (Anglo Saxon word for spirit) would have been with Freyr. He's a god whom is associated with plant spirits. I started a garden prior to his instruction and have a respect for plants in ways many people care not to think about. Working with Green Wights has been a challenge in some areas. They don't speak in the same way that we do. Often times, the way they speak to us is through emotion or personal feeling, sometimes actual energetic vibrations or even physical appearance. They can be difficult to understand at times if you aren't accustomed to their language, and sometimes can be quite vengeful. Other times, they can be quite kind and gentle. My interactions with them, especially with tomato, were very rough. This was mainly due to my parents not having the same ideals and respect for plants as living things. However, my relationship with mugwort is very much a business venture because an offering is given, and in return I get a portion of their limbs to use in recaning (cleansing by smoke). Many of the green wights just do their own thing. Only certain ones work with me on a regular basis. My gardening is mostly for the purpose of helping wildlife, like the ever decreasing in number Monarch Butterfly, or my attempt at helping the bees.

My second experience was with "bigger" wights. These wights have dominion over the elements. These particular wights were of places, not so much things but rather a particular place. I've worked with my local land wight before with grounding. He appeared to me as a giant clay and soil dragon, with no wings. He was big, bulky, and brown. My other experience is with three brothers, whom were introduced to me by Skadhi. The three brothers govern over the winds of my local area and I often call to them by giving them offerings in exchange for rain or even sunshine.

It's important to remember that while I say they have dominion, I don't mean they control the weather or places or forces. I mean that they are those forces. They had chosen to make themselves apparent to me in some way or were introduced to me either by a deity, or by meditation. My relationship with them is not really about business, I enjoy their company as friends and don't just go around them for stuff I want. In some cases, they also benefit from being my friend too.

Many of the plants I work with have guardian spirits who watch over them. They are protectors of their race of animal or plant and help their species survive. You could say they're a parent spirit of that particular species. I've found these types of wights in pretty much everywhere and in everything, including rocks. I once met a wight inside my crystal ball whom was associated with a large crystal cave. For some reason the wight chose to associate themselves as male, but took the form of a giant cave with crystals everywhere. He was very understanding in our interactions and made the passage "safe" for me to travel in when I was learning divination by gazing into crystals.

Respect

Respecting your local spirits as well as the otherworldly ones, is very important. You don't have to have a physical tree to commune with a tree.

Sometimes that tree wight decides to come to you in a different way. This is much like my personal experience with Rowan. Sometimes no matter what, even if a spirit is mean to you, you should absolutely treat them with the utmost respect. They may control powers or forces in which may endanger your life, especially if it has anything to do with luck or natural forces. They are not to be trifled with! Many stories of the fairy are very clear about the rules. Before you go trying to force a spirit into working with you, remember that you are not their master. They don't have to do what you say, and if they do, it's because they choose to. If you have angered a spirit, make peace with them if you can, and try to come up with a solution. Spirits or wights also have connections to deities you may be unaware of. Sometimes when you offend a specific individual spirit, you may also be offending someone else whom they are associated with, and may even make that deity, or other spirit have something against you.

Spirits, wights, gods, deities, they're all really some form of spiritual entity who exist in a different way than we do. Don't assume that just because someone is an elf, a dwarf, tree, etc, isn't also a god. In the past there were household gods, which often related to gods of a place or spirits of a place. A very popular deity many people know about is the Green Man. The Green Man is associated with a group of two others in Sherwood England. The Green Man is actually a deity/spirit/god of a place. It was interesting when my friend who lives in England had given me this information, which further confirms my experience. If you're interested in learning more about this particular subject, the book *The Tradition of Household Spirits by*

Claude Lecouteux is a very interesting read!

Working with Otherworldly Gods

My work with the Norse gods is incredibly personal. I work with Odin, Frigga, Thor, Eir, Freyr, Freya, Skadhi, Loki, and Hela. I'll explain more about my relationships with them later, but for now I'll talk about how it works. Originally, you read in the first chapter about my oath to Odin. Through this oath I also work with the other deities mentioned above. Specific things are expected of me because of my oath. Each deity has something to teach me, and each of those things are important to follow.

Never just oath yourself to a deity! You may end up in a situation where a deity may actually abuse you in some way, or force you into doing things you really don't want to do. While there are many benefits to being a god slave, I don't recommend you just fall into it without first researching things from other people who are in that situation. Most deities have a certain way they like things to get done, I'm expected to follow those ways based on how they present them to me through meditation and trance. If a person requests my skills for a divinitory reading, then I am expected to follow through with it as soon as possible. It's not something I'm allowed to pick and choose, even if the person ends up being really rude or unappreciative about what was said in the reading.

Gods aren't going to make you happy, they expect that to be done by yourself. They'll help you do things if you're willing to do part of the work yourself, but if you are going to be lazy they'll most likely ignore you. There was a situation with a client once where Eir got mad because the person wasn't doing the things they were supposed to. She said she was slacking in her efforts to make herself better, and was choosing to ignore her problems. Let's just say a lot of bad luck followed her until she did what was recommended in the reading that I gave to her.

You don't have to oath yourself to a specific god or goddess to be bossed around either. Sometimes they'll be like "You're mine!" and that's the end of the story. At which point you either have to negotiate terms, or you have another deity run interference. Most of those things don't really play out well for the individual though. Gods do things you don't like, that's the bottom line. Sometimes they don't treat people in a way that most people would expect. Gods don't abide by human rules or standards, they abide by their own accord and personal agenda. If a god comes a calling, you don't always have a choice in the matter of saying "no". Sometimes they just continue to bother you anyway despite what you believe or want. I've met many a people who say they have been repeatedly harassed by a specific deity. With this kind of situation, it's never wise to run away. Sit down with them, pray to them, and just tell them your feelings and concerns. Tell them what you would like and try to negotiate terms or contract where things could work out at a later date. If it has anything to do with cultural differences, perhaps explaining that you don't feel confident enough that you can honor them properly, and that if you can't honor them properly then maybe it's best not to work with them at all.

Refusing to work with a deity is you sitting down and having a chat with them. Don't just run away! No matter where you go, they'll find you and screw your life up until you do what they want. I'm just giving you an alternative to running away, because most of the time running away or just simply saying no isn't enough reason for them to stop. They can be like a serious obsessive boyfriend or girlfriend who won't take no for an answer! So just sit down and explain things and see where everything goes. You may find that they can be quite understanding.

Working with a god or goddess doesn't mean you have complete servitude in them or that you are bound to them in some way. Your interests could be totally different. Which means you can do whatever you want whenever you want. Contrary to popular belief, having a god phone or being able to directly commune with the gods is not exactly a normal thing, even though it seems to be in certain communities. Typically it's something that a normal person doesn't do.

The gods can be rather tricky because they may have their own agenda or their own idea about things. They aren't above learning new things, but may have a preferred method when it comes to performing something in particular. My work with Odin for example is very different than how I work with Freyr. Odin teaches me about will, keeping schedule, and achieving trance states. However, Freyr is all about the land, working in a physical way with plants and animals that allows both sides to benefit from each other. Two completely different types of working, yet at the same time, still honoring and being true to said deity. However, there's always the fact of being able to work out your problems or disputes with them by simply stating that you can't do something because it's outside of your means to do. If they still want you to do something in a specific way then you should ask them to provide you with the means to be able to do it.

The bottom line with working with any spirit or deity is communication. It doesn't matter if you have to go to someone else in order to speak with them. Attempt to make a conversation and work with them in a respectful and honest way. You'll go far by just being respectful and honest. I have a friend who seems to always be rude to the gods and goddesses she works with, yet everything she says is honest, so she is respected by them because she tells them exactly like it is. Sometimes, even if you're rude, they respect honesty and the fact that you had the guts to stand up to them in that way. They view people very highly if you're able to hold your own in a conversation with them. If not, then you may be treated unfairly and poorly because they may see an opportunity to take advantage. Like I said, they operate under different rules and guidelines, and it's best to just be cautious with any deity who comes your way!

Chapter 3

Seidr

Seidr is a form of sorcery often mentioned in Norse lore. I focus on the trance states of Seidr to help me perform divination as well as speaking to deities. When I go into a trance, I am usually performing some type of service for people, or I am speaking with a god or goddess. Don't take this the wrong way and think this experience is amazing and fabulous, it couldn't be further from the truth. Most of the time, what I see is like a dream. I am still very much aware of my physical body, but my focus and consciousness may be elsewhere. How do I know it's real? Usually there's some form of encounters, like clients whom I have done long distance healing for have said they felt something happen, even when I never told them I was doing it.

The purpose of Seidr for me, is using it to glean knowledge either from someone, or wyrd itself. Wyrd is a very complex strand of information, often times appearing as glowing threads that connect people to things like their car, a friend, an accident, a situation, etc. Wyrd is the fabric which makes everything happen, and it can be directed by certain deities or spirits. When I perform divination with cards or runes, I will often dive into wyrd. I essentially plug myself into a force that's much more vast and wide than I could ever be. People have said that when I enter this state of consciousness, I do not sound like myself. They tell me

I sound like someone or something else. I write everything down in a journal, then I speak it aloud to my client. Sometimes what I get is from a deity, other times it's from the spirits in the cards or runes.

I will most often forget an experience I had when in a trance state. I may recall certain words or even events I saw or heard. I may recall the initial experience and flavor of it, but I may not remember the exact words or even anything at all. It various depending on the situation. First starting out with Seidr however, I got massive headaches. These headaches would last for a period of months and always after I performed some form of Seidr rite when speaking with the gods. It had a physical sensation to it. It felt like a big hole was in the back of my head, right where the spine and skull connect. It was through that hole that I could actually feel things "move in". (When I say things, I mean words, knowledge, etc.) After a time of experiencing this, the headaches disappeared and I was able to enter trance with no pain, but always with the after effect of feeling drained.

Grounding is very important in my working with Seidr because it helps me to feel less unbalanced. This means that if I don't ground, I may get headaches, dizziness, to outright fatigue. There was one day I didn't ground, and a few minutes later, I collapsed on my bed going to take a nap, then I slept the entire day and still felt tired afterward. I began to realize that grounding is essential if I want have a foothold in this world. Not grounding would mean that my energy reserves would deplete themselves repeatedly, no matter how much I ate or tried to stay awake, the trance-state was working against me.

I have had many experiences during Seidr.

Through my initial contact with deities, they would often meet me in a place that had been created by Odin for me. It was sort of a way-shrine where I could safely meet them between our world and theirs with no problems. It was there that they would often impart their wisdom and techniques down upon me through a series of unusual acts that would lead to some form of new "ability." Like Freyr would suddenly appear and shove a seed into my chest, and then I would be able to talk to plants. These experiences were often trials, and in some of them I would actually feel a physical pain from the whole ordeal.

Method and Details

Many people favor the high seat or other people chanting around you. Those methods don't work so well with me. How I learned Seidr was through a training process that I gleaned from Odin, Freya, and a few books. None of the books I read taught me an understanding of how it works, it was something I had to experience for myself. It was just breathing in four, holding for four, then releasing, and repeating again. I would do this over and over for a few years before I actually got a handle on how everything works, or at least a vague idea of how it works. If you want to learn Seidr, do not expect immediate results in understanding the mechanics of the magic that is involved. In fact, I recommend you actually go to a deity first and request for them to teach you. This is mainly due to the protection they can offer you. I'll be giving you a rundown of exercises however, at the end of this chapter.

If you want to learn my practice with Seidr, you

should start with the breathing I mentioned above. Allow yourself to focus on that breathing. Do this every day of the week at a specific time. The more you do it, the more you will be accustomed to drifting into trance. Allow all your thoughts to filter through. Don't try to force your thoughts away because that may not work. Allow whatever thoughts, chatter, situations you were dealing with, etc, to just come through your head. Eventually, you will lose all train of thought and begin your decent into a trance-state. You should probably do this for about five minutes everyday and increase the time five more minutes depending on how you feel about it. You can also try listening to music, playing an instrument, recordings, or even use certain herbs to help you achieve a trance-state. Seidr is a type of magic you have to learn gradually, at least in my experience. It's recommended to have an understanding of grounding and spirit working before you even attempt it! If not, you're bound to run into trouble!

Once you actually achieve a form of trance-state, you may notice that you're just sort of stuck inside your body. If you want to journey then you'll have to learn to get up out of it. What you need to do is have a sense of yourself. It means you need to start with visualizations and know what your body looks like. You need to be able to get up consciously, but without moving your body. Performing the breathing technique I mentioned earlier will help to release your spiritual body from your physical body over time. All you'll see at first is just darkness. Once your mind is clear from all distractions, and if you just allowed your thoughts to become that way over time, then you'll see that you actually have control of where your consciousness goes, even if you hadn't been there before. When you do this and you have an idea of where you are going, or you are being guided by a deity, then you will end up where you need to go. If I am traveling long distance in this world, and I know where my final destination is, I can easily travel there. If it involved another world however, there are often portals involved that I have to enter, then paths are provided by the deity whom I might be going to speak with.

Other worlds, like Asgard, are heavily protected. You can't get in unless you have an authorized invitation. Heimdall has never let me pass into Asgard unless I had a scheduled appointment with Odin. They're very private, so most of Asgard was actually blocked from my sight. Other worlds are dangerous, and you always run the risk of being harmed unless the deity you're working with makes sure you arrive there safely. Which is why it's always a good idea to have that initial protection from them.

You should have a purpose you're trying to achieve with Seidr. You shouldn't be practicing it because you think it's cool or awesome to do. Not everyone can commune with the gods when using Seidr. Some gods require more of something else to speak to them for some reason. However, there are other purposes for using Seidr. Seidr can be used to view the threads of wyrd, tap into someones mind to confuse them, or sometimes help them. Seidr isn't always about leaving your body and going elsewhere, it sometimes has to do with things within.

Seidr magic is also a type of magic that may involve spirit possession, either by deity or other spirits. Let's just say that possession is very rare and most people can't do it because they lack something or have to much of something. Possession requires that you let yourself go completely to the gods or spirits, and most people can't fathom not being in control. That's why you don't see people now-a-days getting possessed on a regular basis. It's because most people can't do it.   This is where we get involved with the conversation of if someone is responsible or someone blaming something on a deity because they were either told to do something or were possessed at that time. Let me make this perfectly clear. **We are all responsible for our own actions. Even if we are possessed, we still have a responsibility to ourselves and to our body. We cannot blame a deity or a spirit for our bodily actions, even if we were not aware of them!** Gods and spirits live by different rules than we do. They don't have to abide by those rules, we do. If something happens or you make someone upset, then it's your responsibility to make things right! Even if you were under the influence of a deity or spirit, there is still no excuse for you not to take responsibility for what happened. Say you were possessed or whatever, then you found yourself in a car wreck, you would have to pay the fine if you got one. If you didn't then you would go to jail or worse, prison. This concept applies to proper etiquette in social situations too! I know this has a lot of controversy with it but, regardless of the circumstances, you are responsible for your own body and your actions, even if those actions happen to be verbal. Basically, it's not okay to be an asshole.

When it comes to seeing the threads of wyrd, you have to be aware that sometimes the threads may represent themselves as some form of picture or symbology you have to decipher. In my lessons with

Frigga, she taught me the ways of how to see the threads and how sometimes they can be confusing. Wyrd may appear as a tapestry or several strands of light that look like threads. Other times you may just dive into trance and obtain information suddenly once you're deep enough. Sometimes what you get is a strand of information, not an actual deity or spirit but rather the flow of wyrd itself is flowing through you, which can be extremely draining. There was this one time however when I got this message from my friends Grandmother who had previously been trying to get a-hold of him. The things I was saying to him made him very emotional because they were things only she would say. He told me that he knew it had to be her because she was the only person dead or alive that would speak to him in that way.

When you work in Seidr, sometimes you get certain abilities if you are working for a specific deity or deities. They give you access to information or things that normal people wouldn't have access to. This is mainly because it comes with everything they're trying to make you into. Like for speaking to the dead, that's an ability that would be granted by Hela for me. However, when it comes to healing, opening people up by reaching into their spiritual body to pick out shards of a weapon that had been jabbed inside them because they were attacked by a spirit, is more in line with lessons from Eir. At the same time, things regarding trance, out of body, meditation, etc, can govern in the expertise of Odin or Freya. You don't have to have any special attributes or even be a god slave to practice Seidr however.

Dangers and Precautions

There are parts of Seidr that involve divination and there are parts of Seidr that involve journeying, which is what most people call astral travel. This is where things get extremely dangerous. If you don't have proper protection or you just decide you're going to go off into a place and expect nothing will hurt you, you're wrong. Journeying to other-worlds is very dangerous because while you may be a spirit there, you can still be harmed spiritually, which will sometimes effect your physical body. I had this experience once where I was performing a healing rite with a client. There was this orange gunk all over their wyrd threads, like some kinda fungus or infection. Afterwards, I didn't recan (cleanse by smoke) with mugwort, and I developed a rash on my hands because I touched the orange gunk! The rash began to spread up my arm and began to sting and hurt. No matter what I did, it didn't help. When I decided that it wasn't just my imagination, I recaned and the rash went away almost immediately, minutes after even! A similar experience had also happened to me with a fox spirit. The spirit bit me on the hand and a big rash began to form on my hand. It wasn't a very pleasant experience. I had to apologize and make peace with the spirit in order to get rid of my affliction.

Please research all forms of spiritual protection and apply them and if you can, or get the protection of a deity! There is nothing worse than roaming around the worlds and someone decide to follow you home and make a mess of things. These entities don't care who you are or what you do. At the same time, don't make your shields or wards so obvious because some spirits are attracted to big shields and wards and may see it as you're trying to pick a fight. Have a shield for your shields! What does that mean? It means you put up a shield to hide your shields! It's also a really good idea to have multiple layers of shields made out of different materials. Trust me when I say that you'll be glad you did! If you want anymore information about shields and wards, you should get the book *Spiritual Protection by Sophie Reicher.* While some of her ideas are controversial, the book really helped me understand why it's important to have these things, and how to make sure they continue to work properly. It was very eye opening.

There are things that I recommend you have in the practice of Seidr, but you don't have to abide by those guidelines at all. I merely recommend them because of my experience of not having them is bad, and often times will result in a dangerous situation. I mean, it may even be unlikely that anything will happen, but it's better to be safe than sorry. If you choose not to follow by the advice given here, then that's totally fine. They aren't rules to practicing Seidr, they are precautions to prevent something from happening. The bottom line with all of this is that spirit-working in general is not safe, and the more you open yourself up to things by practicing Seidr, the more someone is more likely to follow you home and cause trouble for you. At the end of the day though, you have to decide for yourself of what is right or wrong for you. If my methods of practicing Seidr do not meet your standards or is to restrictive, then by all means make your own guidelines. All I'm offering here is my experience on the matter, so you can take that as it is.

Communing with Gods

This seems to be the topic on everyone's mind. How can you work with a god? In what ways does one become closer to a god? The answer is not a simple one, and it is most often something that everyone wants to do. A lot of people come to me and ask me questions like: "How do I work more personally with the gods?" or "I can't seem to directly communicate with the gods, what can I do to make it happen?" A lot of people aren't going to like this answer, mainly because everyone wants to communicate with them. However, sometimes people are unable to commune with the gods directly. There are a variety of reasons behind why.

Sometimes we have to much control. When it concerns direct communion with a deity, we have to let go of ourselves. It means we have to be able to allow them inside of us in some way. A lot of my conversations with the gods happen inside my head. It's like they "move in" with their divine force, and start talking to me. It took a long time to understand what this really meant, and what it didn't mean. Often times, it feels like I am not alone. It feels very intense, like the air just got a little heavier, but in a really good way. (Although sometimes, not so good way.)

You could say that the ability to commune with the gods falls under some form of brain wiring, but then depending on the situation, that isn't really true. In the past, a lot of people who were labeled insane were said to be worker of the gods. People claim that the madness was the mark of the gods. Today, we know this isn't entirely true, although some may actually have some form of mental or even physical disability.

On the other hand, they say it's either an ability you are born with, or it is an ability that is given to you by the gods themselves. Whatever is true, and each of these answers have some truth to it, the situation is different for everyone.

Odin began to work on me, training me for the task he had for me. In no way was this work amazing or glamorous. In fact, it was down right dangerous. It was also incredibly mentally exhausting. I would find myself getting headaches all the time, like there was a hole in the back of my head. I could feel it there, literally. When I touched it though, it wasn't there, but it was there some how, because I could physically feel it happening. It was all some kind of spiritual woo shit that I still don't completely understand! The deal I made with Odin is not something to be taken lightly. It shouldn't be something you just decide to do because you think it will be amazing. Doing this form of work can be harsh, and sometimes emotionally and mentally draining. I found that it affected my physical body like I had just worked out the entire day. I would get so tired by the end of the day that I had to go to bed early. Then early that next morning, he'd wake me up at seven or eight on the dot. Time to get up, eat breakfast, read, and then do a devotional rite. Over time, other deities came into my practice and wanted to work with me. I treated them the same as Odin. The entire experience changed my life, and I wouldn't change it back! He has helped me to much.

There is no shame in only being a worshiper or follower of the gods. Becoming their slave or their worker, is very hard work. In fact, I hate god-mouthing. I absolutely despise it because of the ridicule and shame that is put upon me when I say "yeah, I work with Odin". I mean, I don't mind doing readings for people, that's totally fine. It's just, saying things that they're telling me to say, it's not something I love, it's not something I really want to do. Yet it's my job, so he tells me. It stopped being about me when I made the deal, lets just put it that way! Now it's about other people, and my religion and practice isn't just for me, it's for people who need the gods help. When someone wants something and they find me and request my services, it's my job to serve them. However, all that is the professional side to Seidr working, not something everyone experiences.

If you do manage to get direct communion with the gods by using Seidr, then you may develop other relationships with them. These experiences may never involve any kind of work with them, but instead just a personal friendship or even romantic relationship. It can be done, but I just have to say it can be a rare ability. Most often, the reason behind why people have direct communion with the gods is usually to serve them, although this isn't always the case! Either way, I think it's something that is very personal to everybody. Everything that I say here has diversity for every person, nothing is set in stone.

The Uses of Seidr

Seidr can be used for various things. Some people can become wyrd-workers. This means that we become diviners in a way. We can read cards, runes, or other divinitory tools, to help us read wyrd. Diving into wyrd is like diving into a pool that goes in several different directions. It often has complexities and channels of possibilities that people may have never explored. On the other hand, we may obtain advice from our gods or their gods, in how to best handle a situation. A lot of my readings involve advice about how someone can improve their situation based on their current choices. If someone has a question, I can use that question as a focal point to sort of "fish out" the information they might be seeking. Sometimes this involves the interaction of a deity, and other times it doesn't. It may also involve information about an individual you didn't want to know about. Sometimes when you get information, it isn't something you or your client wants to hear. It can be a bad thing just as much as it can be a good thing.

Wyrd-working isn't an exact science and it can even be wrong. Sometimes we get symbols or other things. We could have only read one possible thing, and it turns out to be wrong because either we misread the signs, or we read only a possibility of what could happen. I don't personally like readings that involve someone's future. The future is complex, many things can happen, and that leaves room for error, which is unacceptable in this profession. However, mistakes and errors do happen.

The other part of wyrd-working is helping to change someone's luck. Sometimes a spirit may actually be involved, affecting somebodies life. In this case, we go to them, remove the spirit, and make sure the client is clean. Other times, luck may have to do with a variety of issues from the family blood line, to just personal luck in general. I'm personally skilled at removing spirits. I was often plagued by them as a child. I would see dark shadow spirits in the night by my bed. I would see them around my property. I had no doubt that they were probably also the cause of my depression. After a time though, I learned how to remove them on my own. I now provide this service for people. Removing spirits is no easy task, and sometimes it results in the death of a spirit because they don't want to let go.

I've had a few experiences with removing spirits as a profession. It isn't easy to do, and it can be at great personal risk. I have a few tools that are involved with it. It takes a form of trance to do this, which is why I am involving it here. You usually have to have a sense to see if there is a spirit there, or if it's something else. Sometimes things are just mental disabilities and nothing more. On the other hand though, weird things tend to happen with trouble-some parasitic spirits. Like I said, I have a few tools. I have a sword, a knife, and some herbs that I work with as spirits too. I use my knife to cut cords with spirits or remove things from someone's spiritual body.

There was a situation where a parasite had been feeding on a client of mine. They told me that odd things would happen. Things would fly off the shelf, she would hear things. Their children would talk to the spirit and they would catch them doing it and ask questions about who they were talking to. One day their child came down and said that the spirit had hurt them. They called me in, asking for a recaning and spirit removal. I went in, recaned the house, then I began to work on my client. I took my knife and rubbed it against her back, pushing in mugwort to help cleanse the infected area. Then I removed the spiritual bond between her and the spirit. I put protective runes on the doors, and the spirit left the house. Her husband who had left with their children had returned afterwards. I knew he had been very skeptical about everything spiritual, so it was surprising when he said he felt better. They said that their lives had improved several months later, and that the spirit was still gone.

The ability to fair forth, or what most people call astral projection is another use of Seidr. This takes a considerable amount of time to learn and understand. I still don't completely understand it myself. However, it can be a useful skill, especially if a client lives far away. You can travel spiritually to them, and help them at a distance. I prefer not doing this because actually being there is part of the big process of healing or working with a client. There's also the matter of presence, and being able to sense if a spirit is really there. I mostly fair forth when the gods may call me to their hall. It isn't something I do a lot. Often times, I only go where I need to go and usually, the deity provides the path for me to travel on. You can actually get lost when you're doing it, and it's never a good idea to just go anywhere you want. Even if you think it's all in your head, you may find that you are actually also somewhere else. I had an experience once where I thought I was inside my head. I went into a sacred grove with lots of animals and spirits around me. Then these shadowy men came out of the woods riding on what looked to be boars. One of them, I'm assuming the clan leader, had a large antler headdress on. He told me to leave because the place was under their protection. Where ever it was, it wasn't for me to be. Respect goes a long way when you're dealing with this kinda work in Seidr!

Seidr also deals in matters of possession. It isn't something I have a lot of information on, because I have never been possessed. I can tell you that possession is incredibly rare, and that most people who claim to do it are probably lying or don't understand what possession truly is. It won't be like on the movies, but it can still be incredibly dangerous for the person doing it, and for everyone else surrounding the rite. I've read stories where people would actually chant and act as a battery source. Then there would be a person sitting on a seat or high place. The people would then call upon a deity to enter into the person as they chanted. When the person became possessed by the deity, they would answer questions from the audience or choose people specifically. Sometimes the deity might actually have intercourse with a person or even do something completely unexpected, like try to drive a car. Afterwards, the person who was possessed would often be totally unaware of what happened. In some cases, they may have an inkling of what happened, but the details may be fuzzy. Some people say that true possession is where an individual forgets everything. Sometimes afterwards someone might ask them what something meant, and the person might say something like "Heck if I know!". Either way, I think the experience is different for everyone. There are also different stages of possession that have different affects on people.

I've found that when I do readings for people, I will often forget everything I said. If a deity happened to come in at the time, I may forget what was said unless I write it down. Usually runes or spirits talk to me in readings. I guess in some ways it's like possession, but more often it's like an oracle channeling. I'm still in control and aware, but I am the channel that spirits and gods can use to speak to people. The difference between an oracle and actually being possessed is the fact that when you are possessed, you lose control of yourself entirely in most cases. I've never lost control of myself!

Sometimes Seidr is also used to affect the minds of people. Usually this is through some kind of frenzy that can be brought on by working with gods. The purpose of this is to scare enemies, to make them see things that may not actually be there. It's a mental perception of sorts where you affect the mind of another individual. Typically, I think this alteration in perception was often brought upon by Odin and his dealings with war and rage. Either way it's an interesting form of practice to incorporate, because it makes protection magic included into Seidr.

Seidr is a very complex form of magic. It isn't exactly a singular thing. What I have provided here are merely my own experiences combined with other things I have read about Seidr. In no way should it reflect or be viewed as an all out way to practice Seidr, or represent any other personal practice but my own.

Performing the Rite of Seidr

What you'll need is a place to start at. If you're indoors, you can use your closet, or a dark room. Darkness can be an important part of learning how to perform Seidr because there are less distractions. However, it's worth mentioning that Seidr can and should be performed around noise or quiet places. The reason for this is because you will be able to dive in at any time. Practicing in both gives you more flexibility in the performance. It means you'll be able to go into a trance while you're outside. In which case, if you do decide to go for a more wild scenery, a park would be a great place to go, or perhaps a cemetery. Whatever place you choose, it's important to look at your surroundings. Will you be safe in this place even if it's noisy? Are there any dangers of performing this at your current location? These are important questions you should ask yourself, and all of them need to be addressed accordingly. What is important is not being disturbed. Many things may actually disturb you, but while you are learning how to perform Seidr, you need to be able to not let those things bother you. Make sure no one needs you to do anything, because once you start, you should make it a habit to never stop until you're done. Allowing yourself to be in an area with lots of noise can be beneficial. This is mainly due to the fact that you can attain a spiritual focus, which is needed for this type of magic. You can either lay down or sit with your legs crossed. I prefer sitting up because it helps me not to fall asleep, which is pretty common when you perform trance.

Exercise

Remember the breathing I told you about earlier. Take in slow deep breathes. Close your eyes and allow those thoughts to flow through you. Breathe in, hold for four, breathe out, and hold for four. Repeat this process over and over. Focus on your breathing. Listen to the cars, birds, or people going by you. Just keep your focus on the breathing. If counting is difficult, you can breathe to the rhythm of your heartbeat. Every four beats, breathe in or out and hold each time before breathing again. Let your mind settle, see the darkness behind your eyelids, and let yourself drift off into trance. Relax, no matter what is going on, slow everything down. Remember the scenery that you saw before closing your eyes, if any. If anything has happened recently, allow it to play through you. Let everything move like a stream in your head. Let it pass in and out. Over time you will notice that you are no longer focusing on your breathing, it's okay. Just allow it to happen. Relax, let your mind be put at ease, and then after about five minutes, ground yourself firmly by using a root exercise. This will allow you to come back into a state of awakened consciousness. Repeat this entire exercise everyday or occasionally through out the week. Have a specific time set aside if you can. Eventually your mind will become disciplined the more you practice. The overall goal is to create a mentality, so you can easily access trance at any time. Doing it everyday trains the mind into a specific discipline so you can do this.

Using Seidr with Divination

I typically use cards for this, but you can take whatever form of divination you like and modify it to your liking. I like to use cards because it's relatively easy to do, and it isn't time consuming if you're helping a client. You should have an established form of how to perform Seidr on a whim if you have been doing the exercise mentioned above.

I shuffle my deck as much as needed. Then I take my cards and spread them out in a straight line. I like to have them overlap one another, just because. I have a particular question in mind that I want to ask. This question will help me to dive into trance, and into wyrd, so that I can speak with spirits of the cards, deities, or other entities. The cards work as a medium between me and them, and they can influence what I get with this method.

I place my hand over the cards, waving it from left to right, then right to left. I whisper, or ask the question in silence. Once a feel a tingle on my middle finger, I lower my hand down to the card and pick it up. I then begin to use written meanings for the card as well as my own personal interpretation of the feeling I get off of it. In every reading I do, this is the method that I personally use to ask direct questions. I am in a light trance at this point, and may even receive specific messages from deities or other spirits. Often times though, it's the spirits of the cards who are telling me what is in the wyrd. For me, it comes as a translation through English words, though sometimes it ends up as a feeling I have to decipher on my own. I may get visions along with feelings, or even have a specific conversation with a deity or client. If there isn't a specific question, I have a home made card spread that I created with the help of Freya. I then use that to help me get an overview about someone's wyrd.

End Notes

It's important to keep a foothold in this world and the next if you are to perform this type of work with Seidr. If you keep your practice up with it, you can get really far. Having the help of a deity makes the experience gets even more intense. I hope this helps you to develop your own personal practice with Seidr. Feel free to use whatever I have here and modify it to your specifications. What I have learned about it has taken years for me to truly understand, and there's still more to learn. The gods know the secrets to Seidr, so working with them on it can be very beneficial. Even if you can't commune with them directly, they can help you by sending you moments of insights if you perform regular meditation with them. Seidr is a powerful form of sorcery that can help you develop relationships with spirits in this world, and the next. The practices here may be different than the written lore, but it does put it in a modern in context for you to understand. This has been my personal experience with Seidr and the personal knowledge I gleaned from both Odin and Freya. I hope that this is helpful to you as it has been to me.

This isn't a practice that has long been established. This is a practice that is specific to me and what I have learned. It's a modern way of practice, and using my previous experience with magic to practice something a little more ancient. A lot of things from the past cannot always be applied directly as they were. Either because it's inappropriate, or it's to vague. This is an attempt to revive Seidr as a modern practice by working with the gods. Please remember that everything mentioned here is based on my UPG, and in no way reflects the lore written about it.

Chapter 4

Galdr

As most are aware, Galdr magic is usually performed with words, statements, and overall speaking. Generally the caster would speak in poems. Now a days, almost any kind of speaking will suffice to create a proper way to cast. Galdr is casting spells, meaning that your words have power. Unlike other forms of spell casting, Galdr uses verbal vibrations along with emotion and power of the will to create an effect. Usually a Galdr casting is sung through a song of sorts and felt with emotion and pushed by the will. Almost anything is possible with Galdr, from cursing, healing, and so on.

Galdr can actually be combined with Seidr and Runic magic. While Seidr focuses mainly on trance, a Galdr song can be performed to help one enter trance. Runic magic is also very unique, as you do not just deal with symbols of the runes, but their names as well. The names of the runes can be chanted in Galdr to create a specific effect, which is associated with that particular rune. Combining runes and Galdr means that you are combining your own power with that of the rune, which can also make a extremely powerful magical ritual in and of its self. Galdr can also be combined with different musical instruments. Although this is more of a modern invention, it can still be used just as effectively!

Have you ever felt a feeling when you hear a song, or when you sing one yourself? Have you ever felt that intensity inside you building up? Have you ever felt such a strong emotion when hearing a song, or singing one that it makes you cry? When we Galdr, we create a vibration, and if that vibration is strong enough to bring about an emotion inside of you, then you are accessing part of your energy, that inner most deep energy which makes you who you are. When you Galdr with who you are, you can make things happen, either within or outside of yourself. Essentially you're accessing part of your soul, the inner or higher self as it were. This this is what powers part of the Galdr magic. Galdr magic is specific to vibrations, not just general sound, like the beat of drumming or the whistle of the flute but, it is also the voice. It is power of the voice, realizing that your voice has power. When you speak with your voice and realize what you're saying, you are speaking in Galdr. When voice affects someone with tremendous emotion, that is also Galdr, maybe unintentionally but, still a powerful weapon that most people use everyday.

When you perform Galdr magic, it is to speak with the voice, to allow part of your inner self to access your voice and through those vibrations and emotions, the magic creates the effect that shall be. When you use the power of Galdr, you must be mindful of what you say and do because this means you must also master your voice. What you say might come to pass, it might also affect people in ways that you didn't realize. This is why it's important to collect yourself properly. While we already do this on a daily basis with our mundane lives, there is one thing you must be aware of. Galdr is mastery of the voice, it is being aware of your voice, your words and the actions you perform by speaking. It is a powerful form of magic, being able to control your voice on a whim, being able to realize what that affect it will do once it is uttered.

This may sound ridiculous, but if you have ever played the game Elder Scrolls: Skyrim, you'll know what I am talking about. In that game, you are the dragonborn, you have power over the voice. Galdr is very similar to this. I've noticed that the way the Greybeards work in that game is very similar to the way Galdr can work. (Although, that doesn't mean you can shoot flames from your mouth!) To work with the voice is to take whatever name or words inside of you, making it become part of you. When you do this, you start to master your voice and come to a realization of just how powerful your voice truly is. Even on an everyday basis, we can offend or please with our voices. Galdr is true mastery of the voice, being able to to control what you say, how you say it, and to express your voice with feeling through words or song that vibrates outward to create the magic we desire.

A whisper can be a powerful thing if you know how to channel your will and emotion to achieve the desired effect. You can use Galdr in shielding, warding, and various other things that may require a full blown rite. You replace all that by speaking in words of power. All you need is an intention, a sense of will power, and some emotion to make it all come together. Galdr may seem simple, but it is very powerful!

Chapter 5

The Elephant in the Room

Harassment

There's a lot that can be said about the heathen community. We have re-constructionists, and people who practice with UPG. There are people who only work with Aesir, Vanir, or Jotunar. Some of us even work with all three tribes of gods in the Norse pantheons, such as myself. Others call to the Anglo Saxon gods. Sometimes no matter what paradigm you come from, or what group you belong to; there are issues that rise out of the cracks between people. Everyone has their own ideas, their own insights, their own way they work with the gods. When our beliefs become so important to us that we decide our beliefs and way of practice is better than someone else, that is when we have a problem.

Many people dislike what I do. I claim to be able to speak to gods directly through Seidr. Sometimes that strikes people the wrong way. They think it means that I think I am better than them or that I must think I am special. The reality is that I don't. No one is more special or amazing or better than anyone else. There isn't some kind of god-like list of why gods bring people up to act as their mouth. It's not something I am proud of, it's not something I want to do. I do the things I do because I made an oath. When you tell people that though, they get very upset. Don't get me wrong, I see the reasons behind why. Plenty of fakes exist, plenty of people pretend to have abilities that they don't in order to con other people to get money. It's always wise to be skeptical about someone's abilities. You never know when someone might be trying to pull a fast one. Not to mention that you can't really prove that someone has them by any scientific method. The only real way we have is through divination, and even that can and should be taken with a skeptical eye.

It's not the skepticism that bothers me, because that's understandable. If someone told me I'd be doing this before it started happening to me, I wouldn't have believed them. What bothers me the most is that people have a tendency to overreact about things and say horrible and ridiculous things to a person for the purpose of making them feel bad. They do this because they feel that persons way of religion is wrong, or because they feel jealous about that person in some way. Dictatorship is wrong in religion, and we all should want to learn from one another instead of trying to bash people's heads in.

There was this group on facebook that was saying things about me. They posted my personal pictures on their group, calling me names, saying I was to young to understand. They said I was some emo kid who had no real understanding of the religion of heathenry. For these reasons, I took down all my personal pictures because I felt uncomfortable about people having my picture. What really gets me about this group is that they had the intention of shaming people. That's all their group was about, shaming people who didn't practice their way of heathenry.

I don't understand. Why do people have a need

for hatred against someone who didn't do anything to you? Some people say things like "Oh well that isn't in the lore so you shouldn't be practicing it." You can't dictate your beliefs and way of practice on someone else. It's just not logical in a social sense. Religion is there to give you hope about something and it can be very personal to each person. Heathenry is not an organized religion, and there by does not have any specific rules or established tradition to fall back on. All we have is a piece of work created by a christian scholar who might of put his christian influence into the lore we know of today as the Prose Edda. Not to mention that many of the Asatruar people claim you don't bend a knee to the gods when that isn't even in the lore. Yet they're whining and complaining about how someone else doesn't follow said lore.

It's one thing to say that you don't practice in the same way as someone else and do not agree with it. It's another thing to make someone break down and get emotional and tell them to kill themselves for not practicing in the way you think is right. This is where a lot of our issues lay because people think they have a right to an opinion because well, freedom of speech. Sure, you have a right to an opinion. When you start shaming and blaming however, that's no longer an opinion. That's harassment! I think it's perfectly fine if someone doesn't believe or want to be around me because I practice a specific way that isn't stated in the lore. It's great, diversity is a big thing to me and I like it. It keeps things interesting. However, I'm not going to sit there and let somebody walk all over me or someone else. At the same time though, I'm not going to claim that everything I say is a fact. I will tell someone when something is not part of historical references and when it is. I know the difference between UPG and historical lore.

I had this guy approach me once, saying that what I had on my blog wasn't historical and that I shouldn't be posting it and that I should include in every post that it isn't historical because it confuses people. I'm sorry, but if you don't take the time to read my personal and well thought out about page on my blog, then that's not my problem. I clearly state on my blog that most of my work is through UPG. I don't think that makes me better or more amazing than a re-constructionist because it doesn't. Every time I see a new blog or whatever, I read the about me so I can see if that's a person I want to follow or be interested in. I don't make assumptions about somebody and then come to find out oops, it clearly says right there that that's what they do.

I don't have a problem answering questions from people. I just don't like getting into conflicts with people, especially if we can't just sit down and have an adult conversation. Sometimes in the community, you deal with assholes who think they know everything and want to push their beliefs off on you. They think lore is right and if it isn't lore then you're doing it wrong. I'm sorry but, where is the spirituality in that? Back when the religion was alive do you think they followed out of a book? Of course not! Everything was UPG then when it was happening. What we have today was once someone's UPG in my opinion. This doesn't mean UPG should be the only thing in your practice or that you should only rely on that. It just means that we need to have more respect for one another.

How do you deal with all this crap? How do you deal with people who are harassing you? These are big questions. If it's the internet, there's one word for it and let me tell you, once you do it, you'll save yourself a lot of trouble than just arguing with them about things. Block, Ignore, these are words and buttons we use to stop people from bothering us on the internet. What if my problem isn't on the internet, what if it's in person? Just stop talking to them. Don't even consider being in a conversation with somebody who is only going to harass you about your beliefs. This doesn't mean you shouldn't talk to anyone who doesn't fit with your beliefs! It only means that you shouldn't talk to someone who is only going to care about their opinion and not care about your feelings. Sure, let someone speak their opinion, but when they start disrespecting you by shaming you and other things, that's when you walk away! There is nothing wrong with having an opinion about something as long as they are not harassing you. In fact, even if you dislike what they said, that doesn't mean that should be it. You should respect them and their opinion, to be open minded about what they too believe. At the same time though, you should also stand up for your beliefs. You should just simply say that you don't believe what they believe and that they shouldn't dictate their beliefs off on you or anyone else. Let that be the end of it.

I don't have many heathen friends, but I do have friends who are part of different belief systems. I may speak my opinion about their beliefs, but I do not do so in a disrespectful way. So if my soft polytheist friend starts talking about doing a ritual to the goddess, I don't get offended or upset at her just because she's a soft polytheist. Sure, we may accidentally offend one another sometimes, but it's not like we are outright harassing one another. That's what I am talking about with respect. You can have a civil conversation with somebody and maybe you say something wrong or disrespectful, but you didn't mean for it to come off that way. Don't get angry when they get offended, just say that you're sorry and try to move on with it. When you're talking to someone with different beliefs and you don't want to cause a problem with them, you just drop it. If they happen to be pushing their beliefs off on you however, that person isn't mature enough to handle that type of conversation! At which point, you need to stop and walk away. Your opinion isn't going to change anyone who doesn't want to be changed. You simply tell them they're being ridiculous and you don't want to be around them if they're going to be an asshole.

A Word About Ergi

First of all, you have to absolutely know that I'm a gay male. Why? It seems like everyone is to interested in someone's sexuality. They say anyone who practices Seidr is actually an ergi, which is supposedly some ancient law that states men are unmanly if they practice it. Let me make it perfectly clear to you that it doesn't matter. This law, this term, no matter how it was applied in the past does not apply to modern times. Do we also condone the sacrificing of other people? I think not!

You don't need to bring in mine or another person's sexuality when it comes to heathenry. It's illogical, as it has no place in our religion if it ever did in the past. You can't apply ancient laws or ways of thinking on a religion that has been dead for over a hundred years. It just isn't feasible. So when others shame and all that other nonsense about how I'm gay and I'm practicing Seidr, it doesn't matter to me! In my opinion, if the gods had a problem with it, then they would say so in my meditations with them. If they did then we would have a serious problem and I wouldn't even be practicing the religion that I do now.

While the term has never been brought up to me personally, it seems people try to make it their business. Why are you so concerned with my sexuality? Don't be. It won't change a thing about my religion or what I practice. At the same time, don't assume that a man who practices Seidr is also gay or some other sexuality. There are straight men who practice Seidr, I'll have you know.

Racism

This gets brought up a lot because people have this idea that only people who have European decent, can practice heathenry. Heathenry has been a dead culture for a very long time, there is nothing traditional or right or wrong about it anymore. The rules and ways of that society are gone, and should never be applied to modern day life and circumstances! It's okay to know that they happened and see it as the past. There's nothing wrong with research. However, applying those things to modern day practice is illogical and extremely offensive depending on what you're talking about.

The heathens who use race and purity as a reason to ban people from the religion are usually people who are racist. These people have this idiotic ideal about Hitler at times, and follow the ways of his campaign. This is where most of the racism stands at because Hitler used heathen symbols to represent his ideals of superiority. In no way do these racist ideals belong in heathenry and in no way do those people represent the community of heathens as a whole! People of the past often traded with various regions and cultures. They intermarried with other cultures and had shared relationships.

Most heathens that I know will tell you that the religion is open to all who wish to practice it. I don't personally see anything wrong with someone wanting to worship, or call to the Norse Gods no matter where they come from. Most of the people in the United States often have different people in their family line. There is no way that you can accurately track your families history because at some point, the government records end. With this information in light, we can never truly know all of our ancestors. While I believe it's interesting and cool to track your family history, and even important, it plays no part in my personal relationships with the gods.

Ancestor Worship

This is actually a very big issue for some people. Many in the heathen community believe that you should honor and worship all ancestors, even if they were mean to you. I've read and heard that if you don't honor all your ancestors, then you're not being honorable. Not everyone can or wants to honor their ancestors for specific reasons. Yes, we may be connected to them through blood, but that doesn't mean our ancestors will even like us if we did. Some people actually had abusive parents, grandparents, or just a whole slew of negative people in their family. Nobody wants or should have to be around that. It's wrong to make somebody feel like shit just because they don't conform to your way of belief, just as we discussed above.

Honoring your ancestors can be a very good thing on the other-hand. However, it doesn't mean everyone has the same kind of family as you do, and it doesn't mean they'll be joining that family in the afterlife! There are other ways to worship and honor ancestors. Such as community ancestors whom helped everyone in some way, usually by building a culture or paving the way for something. Some people may also not have a connection to their ancestors for different reasons. My ancestors for example want nothing to do with me. I've tried to connect with them and even read about them in my great grandfathers records. The lot of them are christian, they don't approve of what I am doing, and that's the end of it. I'm not going to worship or honor people who don't want me around. That's just a given, no one will want to do that. People should stop trying to make others abide by their way of practice when it concerns situations and concerns you don't understand!

Relationships with Gods

Everyone has their own relationships with the gods. No matter what pantheon you call to, no matter if it's the same god or goddess, that relationship with that deity will be different. Just like how we interact differently with people, so do the gods. Not everyone is a spirit worker, god spouse, god phone, or whatever. Some people are just worshipers who wish to honor the gods in some way because they feel connected to them. Not every worshiping person will want to work with the gods on a personal level. Not every person can work the gods as spirit workers, god phones, or god spouses do! Just because you're in a relationship with a deity doesn't mean another person will want that. Just because you work with the gods through spirit working or god phoning, doesn't mean other people can or want to. Sometimes there are just pagans who honor the gods in their own way. We need to let those people do what they want or feel what they need to do. We need to stop expecting people to be spirit workers, god spouses, and god phones!

I think everyone thinks that it's common to work with gods. If you actually researched any amount of cultures, you would know that it couldn't be further from the truth. Every culture usually had a mediator in which would act as the mouth or in-between person for deity interaction. They exist all over the world as various titles. If someone can't or doesn't want to do this, then we shouldn't even attempt to make them. If the gods want somebody, that will happen in its own time and its own way. We can always help guide people, but we should never force our opinions and practices on another person. If that person comes to us and wants to learn from us, that's one thing. If they don't want your opinion about the matter though, don't try to stuff it down their throat. It's okay for people not to want to be a mouth or spirit worker. That is a specialty and it takes a certain amount of training anyway. Things like that don't just happen to everyone. It is a very personal experience that does not apply to everyone and it is definitely a serious problem in the heathen community!

Gods are not singular type of people. Like us, they are complex and individual. Like I said above, they react differently to different people. That means everyone may have a similar or even completely different experience than any of us. They're gods, they are so complex that we can't even begin to comprehend what they are like in all that complexity. They choose to come off to us in ways that will make sense to us, or sometimes...not making much sense at all!

Finances

Not everyone can afford a nice altar. Not everyone can make their own things. When someone doesn't have enough money to make or buy their own tools, then we shouldn't shame them for being in poverty or not having a specific skill! Not everyone can afford to give food to their gods. Some people have such restricted finances that they are struggling for every meal. When you wonder when your next meal will be, you don't have enough to put what leftover food you might have on an altar.

Not everyone has an altar. Sometimes people have only their bedroom. Not everyone is old enough to have a specific area in their room to have an altar. Some people will get thrown out if they express anything other than Christianity. By saying you're not taking Norse Paganism seriously when someone can't afford to do much in the religious area, is basically telling them to starve themselves or spend what they don't have. It's illogical. I think the majority of people who say things like this are well-off type people who have a lot of money and think that everyone has the same situation as they do. If that isn't true, then they must be blind to the reality of life because there are plenty of people, homeless people, or others who cannot afford to do the things we all take for granted. It's not right to shame somebody when we don't take their situation or circumstances into consideration!

When I first started heathenry, I started with a bust of Odin, a chalice, and water. Do you think I had the money to go out and buy whatever I wanted? Absolutely not! I still struggle to give offerings, especially food! Not to mention of what you do with the food afterwards. Everyone said that offering water wasn't good enough. What's better than water? Everybody in the world needs water. It is a resource that everyone needs to survive! By saying that it isn't enough is an insult to the god they were giving it to! Even if all that person has is their time and energy to a deity, that's still worth something. If the gods want more, let the gods tell them what to get. Sometimes when you ask them to provide you with the means for something, then it will happen. That's how things worked out for me, but it doesn't always work out the same for everyone else! Understand that everyone's life is different and unique! Understand that everyone's financial situation is not the same as yours and that you have no right to judge them!

Kindreds

Everyone wants to be in a group. They want to feel that interaction between people. It makes you feel like you're not alone in your religion and spiritual practice. Groups and Kindreds can be a great place to talk about experiences and share stories, or lore. Maybe you'll talk about how a deity helped you in some way or just talk about the stories of them in lore. However, there are a lot of issues concerning this part of the community as well!

Not all, but many people believe that if you're not in a kindred, then you are not a real Norse Pagan or heathen. These sort of people believe that everyone can be in a kindred no matter where you are. I'm here to say that not everyone has the means of being in one. Where I live is completely devoid of anything heathen. The only pagans around here are wiccans, and hardly any of them exist in my town. So the chances of me ever finding a kindred nearby are pretty much zero.

There are issues regarding rules in kindreds. If you don't abide by what everyone else believes or practices, then you are doing it wrong and may even be shamed or blamed for something stupid. I've read many a stories on various blogs and webpages about how people were verbally harassed because they said they were a spirit worker or because they practiced a particular way. This kind of behavior is dangerous, especially when it involves matters of sex and gender identity. For some reason, a lot of men have this problem with a strong woman type figure. I think it has something to do with control and their feeling of inadequacy. There is also a possibility of jealousy and contempt for women trying to be over men.

Most kindreds are formed under one specific title, namely, Asatru. These Asatruar may believe that only the Aesir gods may be worshiped or honored. Typically these people are very brash and like to turn everything into a sexual matter. It's mostly the guys who do this, but I have seen some women do it too. I feel that kindreds in general are best avoided in my opinion because I don't feel comfortable being around bigoted assholes who think they're better than everyone else. These people have serious control problems. I much prefer a wide group space that is instead, welcoming to everyone from all forms of heathenry.

How to deal with these issues

I believe that you sometimes have to protect your ways of belief and way of life. When it concerns racism, you should always tell someone that it's wrong. Tell them about how they're disrespecting Thor and Odin because of their double race status. They're both Aesir and Giant. So when people talk about race, it's best to confront them with a firm sense of things. Don't let people walk all over you. At the same time though, don't allow these people to control you and ruin your day!

Walking away doesn't always solve all your problems. Sometimes it can get you into a bigger mess than when it started. Sometimes showing people what your capable of is a good thing, other times it isn't. If you find yourself in a dangerous situation, try your best to avoid any physical harm. It doesn't mean you have to run away from a situation, but it does mean that you should try to come up with a diplomatic solution to the problem. You should always stand up for yourself and your beliefs, but there comes a time when you have to know when to back down. When does it become to dangerous to continue to be in that situation? Especially if there's more of them than there are of you.

Spreading awareness about homophobia, racism, fundamentalism, and such, are all good things. However, when a person has a problem with anxiety and stress, it's better to avoid issues that would otherwise do them more harm than good. If it's me personally, I say what I have to say, listen to what they have to say, discuss it further if I need to, and then just leave it alone. I don't want to spend my whole day arguing about something stupid. People need to know it isn't okay to bully other people just because they're not doing something they agree with. That is when the freedom of speech no longer becomes a right. It becomes an act of verbal abuse. This is a serious issue that needs to be addressed in the community as a whole. In the end, we need only express the truth of where our faith comes from. That the ancient heathens didn't possess those beliefs.

Chapter 6

Invoking the Runes

A lot of people have different ways for communing and working with the runes. Some people give their blood constantly, some people only give their blood once. Some people tattoo them on their bodies. I personally chose another method, brought on by a meditation with Odin. I was taught to invoke the runes directly into me. By doing so, they would be granted a permanent spot within me. I would be part of them as they would be part of me. Here I will provide you with the Elder Futhark runes and their messages to me and their magical uses. I see the runes as spirits, using them for various things and purposes. They take a lot of power to maintain and they only work by certain specifications for me. I have written down some quotes that I received during my interaction with them, though not all possess them. I also have a list of uses for each one. This interpretation is entirely personal, so be aware that this is my personal relationship with the runes. You can use what is here to discern how you may be able to work with them yourself. This is just a personal guide that I have gleaned by working with them, and in no way does it reflect all or any other practices with the runes on a spiritual level.

Fehu

Fehu can help relationships to flourish, either in friendship or lovers. It makes it enticing and wanted; either sexually or lovingly. The power of Fehu can only be measured by ones self worth, because something only has worth if you make it so. Fehu brings what you find is worth something, which varies from person to person. While Fehu governs over wealth and the growth of crops, it can also help what is most important to the individual. It allows for quick transference when used with Gebo. Fehu is passion and helps whatever you are passionate about to grow to fruition. Fehu can represent jobs, work, or anything concerning finances and or hobbies you love to do.

Uruz

"I represent strength of the heart and body. I am the will that causes change in people's lives. I am the one you reach for when all things seem hopeless. My power lays within strong hearts and minds. Each heart is different in its own way. I help those who summon me realize that strength, true strength comes from the heart and not how much you think that you are. I am the survivalists urge and desires, prey and hunter and I help to manifest this inside the heart and mind to prove ones self worth by not how strong someone is but to show them they have the power to change their lives and who they are inside as a person. This journey is rough but can be useful to those who strive to achieve themselves and summon the strength inside to live life proudly and honorably; not for

others, but for yourself and to yourself so that life can become not only easier, but so you can stand on your own to help yourself. Each way is different, but the empowerment and realization I give will help to manifest a better life that is full of quality and worth."

The voice of Uruz was that of a younger man, at least early to mid twenties. Uruz is a rune of strength that can help you over come many obstacles. It is a creative force that breaks down old forms and builds up new ones. It helps you to have courage and inner strength. It can be used to help in healing and make the transgression much smoother. Uruz represents hunter and prey, the force in which all life strives to live. It can help to bring the things you need in life for your survival. It's a rune of personal strength and will.

Thurisaz

"I am strong and I am willing. I am brave and let man fall if he hold me with no knowledge in the dark. For this is not a game that no man can say is fun. Protection comes at a cost when you wok with me. There is no understanding of what you know to be true. All things must be dealt with in kind. So says me Thurisaz."

I think this means that one must work for their protection and that you cannot simply blindly use its power without falling and hurting yourself. Thurisaz is a rune that must be handled carefully; much like a bomb. It can be used as a force of destruction or to create something essential, but either one produces a great passion that cannot be ignored until something is complete. It may also be used for protection. It is a rune of action which can work on a physical level. It helps to strengthen spells and rituals of any kind while also offering protection.

Ansuz

"I am the running mind and inspiration. I can clear the way and destroy it. I take form in whatever guide that you can easily see me in. Usually within the confines of something that is inspirational. I am the act of spell and the words to thoughts spoken. I am the one you seek to understand in all languages. Without sound, vibration, and will, you are half gone. Know that my power has limits, but from within I am the inner voice."

Ansuz spoke with the voice of a younger male. It has the ability to remove or even set blockages. It can focus the will, and it represents the power of will and intention. It can be used to summon up both. It can control energy and channel it, as it is pure energy. It can inspire and move freely, even through boundaries. It can represent a lack of communication or will in a reading, but also that ones will isn't being directed.

Raido

"I represent the ongoing to destinations which may be known or unknown. I am the light which guides the way. With each passing hour I am drawn. I am that never ending journey within and without. I am the sun but I am also the moon, for travel does not stop even if your life is standing still. Each is traveling to a place special as their own. There is no end to this or my

work, but I represent the long journeys one must take in and out of one's self. I am the movement of an individual seeking their place, either in destination or in the self."

Raidho's voice was deep but smooth. The feeling that I got was passionate and burning like the sun but as gentle as moonlight. It was very awe-inspiring.

Kenaz

A rune of fire that can represent creation or destruction. Kenaz can be destruction that helps to create through healing. It can be used to light the way and create fiery passion, to help find things lost in the self. It seems to have a hidden ability to help one illumininate things about yourself and secrets others try to hide. The vision I get from it is very vague, but reminds me of someone exploring a lost tomb.

Gebu

"I have the power of gift. I extend to all parties of involvement that you work with. These extensions are not limited to specific people. In return for ones services & generosity; I give luck and personal insights. An exchange or trade can be anything of value; a laugh, smile, an object, food, drink & of course coin. These things are not to be taken lightly, for they are not a means to an end, but a mutual exchange which is meant to return in favor or to show loyalty towards your fellow kin."

Gebo's voice was calm & smooth. It helps with smooth transactions and speeds the process of them. It makes sure all things are equal in worth. Exchange can range from emotional to material in any reading depending on the runes next to it. Gebo successful transaction in spells or mundane things. It can be used in self sacrifice to obtain insights if used with Ansuz.

Wunjo

"Don't you want to have some fun? Don't be serious all the time, learn to enjoy life as it is. Look at all the things the world has to offer. It's not just about money; it's about family, nature, friends, and things you enjoy doing. Take a look at every natural thing and see the beauty in it even if it's on a street, look at those tees, flowers, bushes, and even all the animals. It should be a joy to look at. Understand that all things need to have some fun. Don't allow yourself to be contained and restricted in the things you love to do. Go out or be with your friends, enjoy your life and bring some excitement to it without burdening yourself. Let go of everything else for a while and just be in that moment of pure happiness and ecstasy till you feel uplifted. Try music or walking; whatever makes you happy, just do it!"

Wunjo's voice was happy and higher pitched like a jester. Wunjo is the never seeming ending joy. It is a rune of joy and ecstasy. It gives one the ability to remove depression and sadness or anything uncomfortable. It brings out things in you and life which are most enjoyable. It can also mean unhappiness, an unwillingness to enjoy life and that you are stuck in a never ending cycle of depression. Wunjo offers to seek your personal happiness.

Hagalaz

"I am that which was here long before any knew of me. I am the cold of the summer and winter. I come bearing change and destruction, warning and mist. In my true form I am known as Ice in the purest form that we are; crystal. Deep inside each mountain lays crystal, just as inside my kin lays the cold of the skies. Everything around you is forgotten and dead but when I come I signal a new beginning. After every hail is a new look and what seems to be destruction is really the cold hard reality of me."

Hagalaz's voice was raspy but like an old man in the cold, in-between deep and high pitched. I feel that this signifies a transformation. The transformation it offers is that of realizing your own faults through a series of events which causes you to realize your actions and the destruction in and outside of you to transform. It may signify stress or worries in your life, hardships that you may not want to deal.

Naudhr

"I am that which is being. I take form in action and cause what shall be to come forth in the form that is most likely. I protect family and their ways, I protect tradition and the ways it is practiced. I am the old crone that sits in the chair providing stories. This isn't a game to be played, for I am one you call to change, but that change may be what you need and not what you most desire. I work with forces that one dares not to touch and I allow distance from them so that one cannot be burned. It is the way of things in wyrd that I

work, making what is most needed come to pass. Do you have the will to summon me? Are you willing to hand your life over to allow change that is most needed? Allow yourself a moment of thought because denial will not be tolerated. When you travel down this road of need, you can never turn back. Wallow in self pity of the actions you take with me but that will not stop what I do or what will become until your needs are met."

Naudhr's voice was that of a older lady. Its abilities govern over what you really need, making things happen according to what you need to improve your life. It's an unstoppable force once summoned. It will continue to work until you and your life has changed according to what you most need.

Isa

"I am the wintery cold, slow and seemingly never ending. I am the frost and snow of the land. I come in cycles of long prolonged stillness. I am the emissary of cold and darkness. I can teach you the ways of stillness, but you must surrender yourself to the cold. You must be willing to fall but yet remain. Understand that this is a pleasure in its self. You must want this stillness for it to over take you and engulf you. Surround yourself in ice so that you cannot be touched and wait for the cycle to end. Know that ice has a cycle and moves. I am the Ice and wind of winter, I am the bridge of ice and the under worlds. I am that which separates you from your normal thinking and brings you to the stillness of cold and ice. Tread carefully on this bridge and understand that slowness is the best route."

The voice of Isa was that of an old man, but I often heard a cracking of ice. When it spoke, it was slow and calm, even a cold feeling drifted over me from the inside. Isa is stillness and can help to achieve it if you desire. Isa also offers protection by surrounding you in a shield of ice. Isa has the power to calm things. Isa also has the ability to alter weather. If you surrender yourself to Isa; in the stillness you will find yourself and inner focus.

In readings Isa can indicate a stillness or calm point in your life. It can also represent depression with unending cycle. If one uses the power of Isa without dismissing it properly then depression may yet come to settle in, or even the need to be solitary. Isa works as the cold ice, alone and in darkness. Isa can represent an in-between time in which you transition from one point to another. This is often viewed as a bridge of ice, which is slippery. With Isa, one can achieve true focus and become solitary. When a focus is achieved, Isa also can act as a shield to protect you, which is strong, unbreakable, and unyielding.

Jera

"I am the ever lasting cycle of all things. When one cycle begins another ends and when one ends, another begins. Everything revolves and circles around. Even the body you reside in has a cycle and what you eat affects it as the year goes by. Everyone's cycle is different, just as people learn and grow at a different pace; so do the cycles of others. A cycle is a season of events which cause change; either in nature or from within yourself. To force a cycle is to cause

disruption. All things have what you would call an automatic timer that kicks in when something or someone ends and begins their cycle. These things are fragile and so we must always encourage one to go at their own pace, for forcing it could only lead to discomfort and disaster."

Jera's voice was that a woman. Jera is a rune of cycle; of nature and of the self. It helps to take up new skills of talent that one has potential for. It can help to bring up one's own abilities through physical or spiritual means but these are a process that may go slow or fast depending on the individual. Jera also represents the turning of the seasons from winter to spring and onward. Jera helps to bring one's skills into fruition that will eventually change and evolve you.

Eihwaz

"The connection between all things has served a purpose long before anyone knew of it. We reached out to those long ago to teach the ways in which are now practiced. From what remains in the stories are the remanence of what is left but there is yet more to it all than that. I am the bridge between all worlds, the ways in which all paths go. I am the connection between all worlds of the great tree. It is ancient and powerful and when you summon me you also summon the tree. Be warned of what gates you open and what pathways you follow, for all have dangers. The light of the gods may light your way but do not stray from the path which I provide. Understand that all information came across from my pathways and so they will again by the will of the gods. Be warned that these are rough roads which are not made safe; leading to worlds

where the fearsome dwell."

It's voice was that of a young man. Eihwaz is a rune of connections, especially connections between the worlds. These connections are what brought us our traditions today. Eihwaz is a rune of pathways, but the paths it provides are not always safe, as creatures from other worlds may be waiting. In divination this could be connections, lines, or even an in-between time. It may indicate one has already started down a path. It may mean a good or bad choice was made to be on your current path, but may also mean a new pathway has opened.

Perthro

"I am the water which spills from the well and yet I am the well which tells all wyrd. While each is different, I make sure that all possess one. For I am the wyrd in which you seek to know and I am vast and filled with many possibilities. The way of this path is not easy; for wyrd encompasses all outcomes for good or bane. Yet I am what you seek for good fortune and power. You hope to obtain the answers which lay within the waters. But, are you truly ready to accept what it all has in store for you? Everything comes to pass. Some things are possibilities and as you swim through life in the well, many things will happen. I show what will or what may be. Are you ready to peer in the well?"

Perthro is a rune of wyrd. Its voice was neither man or woman. Perthro can show what will be or only of what may. It offers insights into our wyrd to show us what might become if we continue down this path. Perthro has the power to bring our wyrd in motion more quickly, and allows us to journey forth within to discover inner secrets. It is also one of the birthing runes; which helps to ease pregnancy.

Algiz

"To go in unprepared is the mind of a fool. Know this; I am the spines in which one cannot break through with force and will strike back on those who seek you harm. I am harsh but yet I am gentle. I am the place you stand from when destruction calls. It is not cowardice to take refuge from within me. It is however a way to escape and prepare for the coming of something. I am that which links you to the all thing, that which provides you with solitude so that nothing can interfere. Understand that I am also the tree and the link between the other worlds, but also I am mostly the link within you. There is not much else I can do, but from within, great power lies in wait in my solitude, for those with the courage to summon it."

Algiz had neither a male or female voice. Algiz is a rune of protection that will hurt anyone trying to break it. It is also the connection between us and the other worlds, for it is not a pathway, but rather the very link within us that connects us to the worlds. It is our connection with divinity. In a reading it could mean one is well protected or one is to protected from things in life, possibly a situation in which you cannot get out of. It also represents a prayer stance in heathenry, as you raise your arms to the sky to pray to the gods. It's not just for physical protection but protection one can use when journeying.

Sowilo

"I am that which is above. I am that which is within. I am the light of the sun and the burning will of the self. I light the surface to this world and all who stand out. I am the force that nurtures all things on the surface. Inside your heart rests the power of yourself and the will to overcome all obstacles. I am the strength and courage that one relies on. I am the force that causes you to keep living, I am that which you bathe in when you walk outside. My radiance and power is great and when you summon me you shall help me to bring these things into fruition."

The voice of Sowilo was female, sounding like a woman in late twenties and early thirties. Sowilo is a rune of will. It helps to bring about courage, strength, hope, and most of all will. Sowilo is the light of the sun and can represent a lacking in personal willpower, or help you to bring it up within yourself.

Tiwaz

"*I am the structure of all which holds social and legal justice. I am more than law and more than the court. I am the force that which binds all things in to justice and right doings. I can uphold justice and legal proceedings. I can demolish ideals and bring about new ways according to he way of the cosmic standing. I am the structure but I am also the destruction of social structure and laws. I can create new ways of law and structure. I can reform all that you know to meet the requirements of what should be and not of what others want; for the victory could be of the opposing side. I will not stand for those who pay off the system, they will be removed. Behold true divine justice!*"

Teiwaz's voice was strong and firm, that of a younger man. Teiwaz is a rune of justice. If a system is corrupt it can change it to be fair to every person. It removes those who abuse the system. It is in favor of neither side, but of true justice, the justice which is fair of everyone's well-being. It upholds a system like a pillar and allows for balance in social and legal systems.

Berkano

"I am the light of a new birth, I am the healing within the body, I am the birch, I am the beginning and the thanks. My power lies over the plants and the physical body. I can heal the most grievous of all wounds, I can create and make new from old again as the seasons change. I take all the negative to make positive and allow for quick healing. I am the guardian of children and a mother to all. I nourish all who may require it and allow for a smooth and refreshing ending to healing. For where there is great pain, I shall remove it and take hold to promote the light and warmth of healing."

Berkano's voice was of a much older lady, but seemingly kind and gentle as a mothers love. I saw her as a living tree, a tree with a face and human limbs, but skin of bark and hair of leaves. Berkano is a rune of healing, childbirth, motherhood, and guardian of children. Berkano acts as a ray of light that shines down like the sun; not hot and dangerous but light and warmth, allowing for an ease of pain and quick healing process.

Ehwaz

"I am not the road or the driver, but i am the vessel which will take you from place to place. I am not the journey but I am the vehicle you will ride and I am your protector and guardian on the journeys you take. From destinations here on this world or to other worlds. I am not your guide, but I am the force which takes you where you want to go. Remember that there

are many paths which lead, but you must know which path you wish to take if you wish to reach your destination. Only when you realize this will you summon me. I shall travel great distances to take you and carry you surely and safely. It is not the nature of the beings of other worlds to be kind, and so I know the way, the quickest and most desired routes to take to lead you to the home of the gods or safely in your bed."

The voice of Ehwaz was as a younger man and is usually in the form of some kind of animal, typically a horse or like a bubble of energy. Ehwaz is a rune of travel. Unlike Raidho, Ehwaz is not a rune that represents just travel but in the way you get there; through a vessel of some kind. It is the thing you ride and it protects you from incoming danger when traveling spiritually. Ehwaz is a rune of connections between people and represents the coming together. It has the ability to take you wherever it is you need or want to go. Unlike Raidho which represents long journeys and destinations, Ehwaz represents how you get to your destination and what it takes to travel great distances.

Mannaz

"There are things which you do not know that I can teach. There are things, skills and know how that you can learn if you allow me to come within. For I am the master of all skills and ways of living, I am the master of crafts and using of tools. When you call upon me, it is to access the instinct to create and to craft, to make things or to do chores. I give you the power to know and understand all things. There is not a single

skill old or modern that I do not know. There is not a single task or word I do not understand. I am the human understanding and the way you think. I am Mannaz, keeper of all human knowledge."

The voice of Mannaz was of a middle aged man, flashes of him were a wizard type of individual. Mannaz is a rune of the human condition and knows many things. It has the ability to help us understand or practice skills more efficiently. Mannaz's power lays within and and is in fact a rune of the self. It can not only help you practice and learn new skills but it can also help you to find yourself and what you are naturally good at. It helps to find who you are and your place in the world.

Laguz

"I am the primal waters of the primordial lands long since forgotten. I am the calm and destructive forces of water in the element and I possess the the power to bring about the waves and rain to fertilize the earth and wash away the land. I am the force you can never tame and I, we are the being of water, neither male nor female, but we exist in both and have the power to alter the minds to bring about change in the most calming and destructive of ways. We are the water and we are the waves, we are the wet physical taste and feeling across your face and we shall not stop at a summons. We shall come in random just as the storm of the sea. Behold the waves of all the ocean and the bodies of water, we are here, we are waiting, but never fear for we are the change you need!"

The voice of Laguz started as female but then

mixed in with male. Its attitude was aggressive and yearning to make change. Laguz is a rune of all water, fresh and salt. It doesn't control water, but it is water. It can create physical or mental changes in one's life and it doesn't even need to be called upon to start the experience. It can force you to see the negative or inspire you to create a work of art. It is unpredictable like the sea, but useful when you're ready to face it all, good or bad, even when you're not.

Ingwaz

"When the ground is fertile, I lay. When the rain comes, I sprout. When the dying breath of winter breathes her icy breath upon me, I wait. In a time filled with laughter and joy; I come again to welcome you. For I am the seeds of gestation and germination. I am the vessel you carry on with power of hidden word and event which only lay at your feet. I am the seed of creation, that which sparks all things into beginning, and that all expresses into the ground as plants or into the mind as ideas. The power lays within, you need only plant your actions as seeds to see them flourish and offer them support now and again. Remember that all things start with an idea, you just have to water it with action and passion."

The voice of Ingwaz was male. Ingwaz is a rune of beginning that may inspire ideas and help with, crops, actions, and circumstances. Ingwaz does not just focus on good beginnings, but bad ones as well. Ingwaz is also one of the runes of pregnancy and helps to make both male and female fertile. It represents that all things have a seed in which it starts from. It's up to you to plant it.

Othala

"Where you go after dark is where my power resides. It isn't through strength of the mind or physical appearance, but through the power and strength of family and kin that helps to conquer all. Family is not simply by blood, it can be by those who stick by you in times of great need. Through this understanding you must know by now that I am where your heart is, that is where a true home lays. Know that love is sacred and can be sexual or non-sexual and the power of that love is what powers me, what contains and provides a safe haven for all who are kin. For those who you have helped and for those who have helped you, but most of all the feelings you share with them are all what I represent, the protection of family and kin. I am the inheritance and I am the love that is universal. I am the symbol of unity between family and kin."

The voice of Othala was male. Othala is a rune which is the protection and stability of family and kin. It represents relationships of all kinds that include romance, friendship, and aquantances. It can signify disruption within these relationships and offer insight about how to best handle the situation.

Dagaz

"The flowing passage of all things knows no bounds, for time is endless as there is possibilities. There is yet no end to struggles and pain and there is no end to new ideas, even in nature. Everything is complex and even the things you know of possess this

complexity. There is no end to it. For I am the beginning and the end of all things. I am the change but I do not change. I am the flowing passing of time from Day into Night and Night into Day. I am the seemingly never ending cycle that continues to move on. I am a new beginning, the end to all your struggles and I am the choices you make to get there."

Dagaz had the voice of a man, deep sounding and awe inspiring. Dagaz is a rune of change. It represents the passing of time throughout the day and night. It is a rune which signifies that a new beginning shall arise. Out of all the destruction and pain we go through, it signifies there is yet a light at the end of the tunnel. That soon a new door will open to reveal a new path and way of life.

Chapter 7

Offerings

There's a lot of different ways that you can honor or worship a deity. It doesn't have to be through objects, food, or prayer. Sometimes it can be through certain acts. Like when I honor Frigga, it is most often through an act of cleaning. Not spiritual cleansing like recaning, but everyday chores. However, food, prayers, and various objects can also serve as a good way to show your respect and thanks to them!

I've found that most deities like something when you buy or make something specifically for them. It should be something personal and well thought out. Not everyone is a craftsman, so don't be ashamed if you can't make anything by hand. You should never feel guilty about not being able to give something that you clearly cannot afford. If a deity wants something specific, but you don't have the money to offer it to them, then ask that they provide you with the means. It doesn't always work, but sometimes it does.

What you give, no matter what it is, should always mean something in particular. You should always be mindful of what you are giving at that specific time. If all you can offer Odin is a journal with poetry, then make it awesome. Don't just write about whatever, really think about it. Put your own emotion and will into any offering you give. Make sure that when you give it you aren't just going through the motions, because then it won't mean as much.

You don't have to have fancy altars or amazing statues to honor a deity! People have this delusion that everyone has the ability to buy glorious statues and build magnificent altars. Go with what you can afford and set yourself on a budget to make room for offerings if you can. If all you can give is a personal space with just a pen or a paper, or something else, then that's all you can do. Don't make other people make you feel ashamed for not being able to setup huge temples in your house or apartment. The point of honoring a deity is to do it on a personal level. That means that what you give may be completely different from what someone else is giving to them. That's what makes your offering different and unique.

If you want, you can always take up a specific skill, or at least try to learn a form of crafting if you really want to. Even if everything ends up failing, at least you tried to make an effort for them. In the end though, offerings are a very personal thing. Some people even offer sexual energy as a way to give something to their gods. If all you can give is your personal time and energy to them, then that's all you can do! I understand being on a limited budget and not being able to afford a lot of things. In fact, a lot of the things I have were obtained over time. A little savings here or there can help, but if cash is really that tight, then it's okay. As long as you explain why you can't give something, then there is no reason why you should feel guilty or ashamed of yourself. There is no shame in being in poverty. I am sure people of the past understood these types of things too!

If you try to offer what everyone else is offering, it won't be as special. It won't be something from you personally. A lot of my offerings are candles of specific colors or scents I personally chose that I thought my gods would like. Yes, I have an established space to honor them, but that took time and effort to build. It wasn't something I just had. When I didn't have it, I said I wanted to build something and that it would be great if they would help me achieve that. Then over time it happened. I was able to build my own personal altar and put the statues I bought on it.

Some people offer blood as a personal sacrifice. I think it's a good thing, but you should definitely be safe about offering blood. Use sterile tools like a lancing device, because you want to prevent infection. I have used a lancing device and put a drop or two of blood in the scents that I offer. You only really need a drop, so don't try to go overboard and cut your entire hand unless you can make absolutely sure that everything is sterilized before you do it. I don't personally think it's necessary but, some people do it anyway. Blood is probably one of the most personal things that you can give!

Others have this notion that you have to offer yourself as an offering. One thing you should always be aware about is, you should know what you're getting into! Sometimes this results into some form of deal. Like: oh hey I'll offer myself to you if you do this for me. Some people think offering yourself to the gods is something everyone should do. It isn't! Once you do this, you enter into a personal contract with them. At that point, they can start messing with things in your life. The purpose of this is usually so that you will serve them in the way that they choose. Don't be fooled into thinking that gods don't have an ulterior motive. Many people have entered into a contract with the gods, only to find out later that they were just a tool, or a thing they were using for their own selfish desires. When you enter into a contract, always make sure you consult a professional diviner, and do more than one reading to confirm it's true. Contracts are serious business, so never enter into one unless you know what you're getting into. That's why offering yourself as a devotion may not be a very good idea. At the same time though, it doesn't mean you'll be taken up by them. It just means that you may not be able to work with anyone else. Don't let these things make you feel less secure about working with them. Working with gods can be a very life changing experience. In other matters, I am very partial to the idea of burning foods. It's not something I do very often because of my life circumstances, but it is something I feel more comfortable with. I dislike the idea of letting food sit there and rot on an altar. I would much prefer that the food be thrown into the fire. The fire acts as a transport system to them. When I first started out however, I would offer Odin water for an offering. Some people would say that water isn't good enough. Excuse me, but every living thing needs water, and when someone comes into your house as a guest, that is what I usually offer them! Juice is also another option for teens or even little kids. Alcohol can be fairly expensive at times. I don't like to just pour the alcohol out onto the ground either. Depending on the type it is, it may affect the soil.

This is another matter we must be aware of when offering food to the gods: Never just allow wildlife to eat the food you offer. The idea may seem very cool or interesting, but it could ultimately harm the environment. Over a period of time the animals may actually lose their ability to forage or hunt for their own food. This usually happens if the children and the children of those children, have been fed by humans in generations. Then one day, you move, or you die, or you just stop doing it, and those animals die because of your actions. In short, don't feed wildlife, even if it is for the purpose of honoring a deity. It is not a good thing! If a species happens to be endangered or hurt, leave those things to professionals. If you do decide to do it despite these warnings, do not do it directly! Do not try to get them to take it from your hand. Often times, relationships with humans and animals can be dangerous. Not only is it dangerous for us, but it is also dangerous for the animals. They have impulses that we don't and if they end up hurting somebody, then they could hurt someone else because they think that human will want to feed them too. In the end, it may result in the death of the animal. Feeding wildlife also causes them to be a pest to other people, so that's something to think about as well.

Offerings can also be a form of apology or to show interest in worshiping a particular deity. Usually offerings have a vibe about them after you offer it to a specific deity. Each deity has their own unique mark, which can be learned over time. I've noticed when I give offerings, there always seems to be some form of outline to it. The outline is the deity claiming the offering for themselves. You also have to be careful about attracting other spirits into your space. I typically use names and call out to that specific deity by a well known name.

Offerings can take pretty much any form. The most common are food, objects, oaths, and blood. This entire book is actually an offering in and of itself to various deities I work with. You'll notice that every chapter after chapter ten, is in fact a devotional to a specific deity. It's a condensed version of my work with them, the prayers I've personally created, and the things I've learned from them. They have helped me a lot in my struggles, and this is one of the biggest offerings I have ever made. It doesn't have to be a published book like this one, it could just be something you wrote for them that you keep for yourself. Most deities like stories, though some are well known for loving them more than others.

The more you get to know your gods, the more you will understand what they would like. At the same time, most of my experiences are usually what I think is appropriate. It's like buying something or making something for a friend. You're not sure if they will like it, but you get what you think they might be interested in. If you're unsure if an offering was accepted, perform some kind of divination on the matter. Cards or runes work. Any card or rune that represents something positive usually means that your offering was accepted. Other times, the gods let you know what they want. In 2014, I decided it was time to get a proper altar for my gods. Odin guided me to the supplies and understanding of how to build one. I built it specifically for him and the other gods I work with. It was a big project that my dad actually helped me with. I burned symbols all over it, then painted those symbols silver.

This altar took a very long time to setup. There's also a storage area inside that opens up by knobs on the front. Any altar, no matter what it is and what it is made out of, has a spirit associated with it. Once you dedicate a space like this to any deity, the space develops a sort of hallowed feel to it. It's like a sanctuary where all of my spiritual work happens. It has taken a long time for me to amass such an array of statues. They are by no means cheap, or easy to obtain. My Hela statue for example was hard to find.

Altars are very popular. Many people sell them and market them for huge prices. I knew I would never find anything heathen for an altar, so I had to make one myself. Being able to make an altar, much less buy one, is not a luxury that everyone can afford. You shouldn't stress yourself about achieving something someone else has. Instead, you should strive to create something for the gods that is by your own circumstance and capability. Someone once told me that they used a brain model to represent Odin. Whatever works, that's what matters!

Depending on what deity you're offering giving offering to, the method may be different. When it concerns food however, I believe that fire is the best way to go! Some people go through a huge ritual with these sorts of things. I'm not one to get all dressed up or buy or make clothes. This isn't the ancient past, it is right now. That means that I live in the suburbs where cars are flying by my house. I dress the way I feel is appropriate, and I just do my thing. I don't feel clothes are needed unless it's something the gods personally specify. I believe attitude is more important in a ritual than what you're wearing. If all you got is a tank top and shorts, and it's a very hot day, then that's the way it is.

In the end, what you decide to give is your personal decision. Nobody has the right to judge you on the choices you make. Offerings are a very personal thing! They should never be taken lightly or forgotten. No matter what an offering is, it should always be filled with emotion. An offering is a gift to the gods, and whatever that gift is, it should always be treated as sacred.

Chapter 8

The Tribes of Gods

The Aesir

Everyone knows about the Aesir and who they are mostly associated with. Odin, Frigga, Eir, Thor, etc. They are a tribe of gods that often times focus on the production and evolution of nature and humans. Since it was Odin who brought me into heathenry, it's only logical that I would also be associated with the Aesir the most.

The Aesir are usually very proper, they love schedules and are very private people. They don't believe in things like marrying your sibling. Often times, they think they are right about something more than others. They believe that everything they do is of their own right and have a tendency to claim things and people for themselves. They often live up high at the peak of Yggdrasill in Asgard.

I've only been to Asgard a few times, seeing the long white stretching wall and gate. I am often greeted by Heimdall and I am not permitted to see much of Asgard's scenery. I've only been to Odin's tower a few times, where he would often speak to me about important business regarding the tasks he had set me for me. Odin's tower is where he looks out upon the worlds in his chair. The way I saw it was in a cylinder room that lead down into a stairway to the rest of the hall. Inside the tower however, there were three or more "windows" that had a sort of frosted glass design.

These "windows" would actually project images for him to see in multiple places at once.

You could say that the Aesir are very stuck up about a lot of different things. Odin is very protective of his family and his people. He will do anything to protect them and himself from oncoming threats. For this reason, Asgard is not open to the public unless stated by a deity from there. They have a lot of security detail and they make sure no one enters the realm without their permission. This is why entry into Asgard is strictly by invitation only.

Asgard is a fairly clean and bright place. They have places of market and trade there. They have different homes for different deities and battlefields. The Aesir are very proper people, having an etiquette about everything. Not all of the Aesir are interested in human relations. Some of them are very shy and prefer to keep to themselves. I haven't had to many experiences with going to Asgard, but I can say that they seem to have a place for everything and everyone.

The Vanir

There isn't a lot of lore established on the Vanir gods. This could be because the people who wrote it didn't think that farmers and traders were very interesting. However, the Vanir are powerful gods and goddesses in and of themselves. I've noticed that they aren't very aggressive and enjoy simple pleasantries. Although this doesn't mean they can't fight. Many of the Vanir are very capable of protecting themselves and others they care about. They live in various tribes in Vanaheim.

I've never seen Vanaheim for myself, as the majority of that world seems to be blocked to me. This is probably due to my association with Odin, and the tricks he likes to play on the various tribes of gods. However, I have gotten to know Freyr and Freya fairly well. I have gotten feelings from their father Njord. He's a very nice man with a salty sea breeze kind of smell, white hair, and very gentlemen like. I've also had dealings with their Queen and had asked him once before if I were to write a book, if he would inspire me to do so. That's right, I said he. The Queen of Vanaheim is a male. He's very interesting and likes art, music, writing, etc. The Vanir you could say enjoy art of all different kinds and promote self expression.

I can only tell you what I've read from others about Vanaheim. They are a type of elven race that many call the Eshnahai. They work with farming and various animal types. They can be very wary of those wishing to expose their inner secrets, and often do not trust those who work the Aesir. This is why my contact with them has been mostly blocked, except by the big name deities of Vanaheim.

The Vanir are strongly associated with colors like gold and white, although they do like other colors too. They are all about abundance and beauty. They help things grow and accept things as they are. Yes, they are agricultural, but they are so much more than that. They are craftsman, warriors, farmers, wyrd workers, and healers.

Freyr taught me a lot about how to harness ones inner abundance where as Freya taught me how to dive into my spiritual body. (aka, astral form.) There are a lot of great things that can be gained from working with them, but that shouldn't be the only thing on your mind. They are just as powerful as the Aesir, and just as dangerous. They just have a different approach to things.

They can help bring things out from within you. They can see the potential deep within you and help you build yourself up to something better. Much like how a plant is tiny when it sprouts, they can help us to flourish and prosper. They're associated with sex and do accept rites of sex as offerings. They have a tendency to see the potential in everyone and everything. Beauty isn't just all shiny and wonderful things, sometimes it's the dirt and smelly decay. Hard work means something to the Vanir people. They enjoy teaching you something if you're willing to do all the work required for that skill. They're not pushovers and will not always take no for an answer. I may have thought I couldn't do something, but working with them has often proven to me that I can.

Everything you do with them has a bigger purpose. A lot of people don't like the idea of a weed-full garden. Freyr wants me to appreciate the overall sanctuary that I have provided for other beings around my area. Not just the pretty ones, but the annoying ones too. Stepping into my garden is like stepping into the woods, mainly because it's filled with weeds and various other plants I've planted. The Vanir can teach you the ways of plants, or decide to help you learn about animals, or they'll show you that hard work makes you achieve something in life. Each skill you learn from them will not be easy. Even if that skill is gardening or wyrd working. You'll notice that each skill has its own specifications and difficulties. However, with hard work and dedication, you too can achieve great things. You may learn to appreciate the natural beauty of everything around you. Most Vanir are egalitarian and treat everyone as equally as everyone else.

The Jotunar

The Jotunar live in various places, not just Jotunheim. They live within the frosty world of Niflheim, and the scorching volcanic world of Musplheim. The Jotunar are giants and they possess many powers of shapeshifting. When they shapeshift, that isn't just something they can do, it is part of who they are. They are very similar to elementals, but at the same time they are not. They can adapt to their surroundings by changing their form. They are associated with all forms of life from natural disasters, animals, plants, various weather patterns, and sometimes the very earth itself. Many of the Jotunar are very savage, primal like beings. They would more think about eating a human than working with them. Many of them also want to work with humans for various reasons. They have a short temper, and can be angered easily. They mostly dislike excuses and trickery. If I have learned anything from them, it is that they believe everyone has worth. That anyone is capable of hard work in different ways. They tend to see no reason to work with anyone who isn't willing to put forth the same effort that they put out.

They will often end up shunned in most groups because people believe they are evil. Evil is a term that cannot be rightly placed upon any given spirit, especially the Jotunar. They are powerful beings just like the Aesir or Vanir. They can teach you the ways of hunting, or discovering and working with your primal self. They are the brutal parts of nature that no one tends to like. The lessons they have to offer are ones that often involve survival.

My only experience with going to Jotunheim was through the will of Skadhi. She allowed me safe passage by guiding me to her residence. It looked very vast and wide. It was night, in a mountainous tundra. Jotunheim is a large world, literally meant for giants. The snow was falling down a bit, and I saw the sky lit up in stars. I have only ever been able to visit there a few different times. It's not exactly the most friendliest place to go. Jotunheim has a lot of dangers if you're not being guided. I don't recommend going there without a guide of some sort. Either a deity who lives there or someone else who knows the area. I was only allowed to see certain things, then that was it. It's not a right to go there, but rather a strict privilege, or so it was with me personally. I don't think that all of Jotunheim is snow and mountains. I saw forest in the distance.

Chapter 9

Odin

Odin The All Father is dangerous and cunning. He is quick witted and will trick you into doing something for him. Then later you might get murdered or something odd will happen to you. It's funny because while people talk about how the Giants are evil, they fail to realize just how dangerous Odin is. That he'd do anything to get what he wanted and more. He doesn't care who gets hurt in the crossfire of his own desires. Not to mention that Odin himself is part giant too.

He is all about schedules and keeping to them. He likes things to be set at a specific time and he likes me to read and write about things. He likes me to get involved with crafts, making my own tools and sort of letting that experience guide me to make something spiritual. He's very specific about detail and wants me to think about purpose. Yet, he's also very open to different ideas and likes me to be open minded about everything. He seems to be very adamant about how knowledge is important, and how even something false can contain some form of truth or knowledge. He can inspire people if he chooses to. It isn't just poetry that he works with, it's every word, every written word he seems to take interest in, and the power that those words may contain. All knowledge is important to know. It doesn't matter if it's something new or old. He doesn't just specialize in all knowledge. He's about every craft and how to, every little puzzle. He can infinitely teach because he has gathered so much information and how to work it that he can do almost anything.

Odin has taught me a lot about myself, and about learning and acceptance. No practice is wrong, because each brings something new to our practices. He teaches that we must learn to absorb all forms of knowledge. To form a collective of information that is filled with even the seemingly most insignificant of things. All knowledge can be important depending on how you look at it. Nothing is below the other. Everything has a purpose.

Odin often gives me the vibe of a headmaster of a magical school. In the beginning, Odin helped me to focus more on studies, making my focus longer and more productive. This focus was needed because I had, and sometimes still have a hard time reading for long periods of time. He helped me to grasp focus and obtain the ability to read longer. He is associated with reading, learning, acceptance, personal change, and adapting to different situations. He is associated with the written word and is master of languages. Odin is not just a god of many names, he is also a god which can transcend into different cultures. When we move from place to place, he can help us adjust to that specific area of culture. Every state, town, city, country, and area in which they reside has a specific culture that may differ from other areas. No one culture is entirely the same, no matter what state or country you live in. Each place has their own quirks and identity. Odin transcends all of those things because he is a wanderer. He goes around many different places gathering knowledge. Odin can make a disguise that best suits to the area of a specific culture. He can also help us to imply this sort of behavior into our lives because he can teach us how to change, and how to be what we need to be to fit into a social standard. This comes in handy when you are in a workplace. You can't just be who you are sometimes in a workplace. Odin can teach us how to put on different disguises and access different personalities within ourselves. This also governs under self growth and it helps you understand the complexity of yourself. When we take upon this change, we take it into our very being. When you act a certain way and do things a certain way, it becomes who you are in the end. It doesn't mean you're being a fake person. Not when you have adapted to that specific behavior. It's only fake if you are not passionate about this form of work. If it doesn't change you in a way that betters yourself then it's not the same thing. This change is natural and can either be easy, or difficult to adjust to. Either way, Odin teaches us how to express who we are onto others with better clarity. These of course, **are not** aspects. They are things inside of us that he helps to manifest. It can be something you dislike or something you don't mind doing. He teaches us the ability to accept change not just on the outside, but from within.

Odin has many names. With each name he takes upon a different personality. He chooses to change himself for the better in order to continue on his journey for absolute knowledge. To do this, he must change not only who he is, but how he acts and perceives the worlds. He is part of that all encompassing cycle where the mind evolves into various other things but yet, all these things are part of him as a whole, they are not separate from him in any way. It is only his personality that we believe has changed. Do we not change to better suit a situation that calls for unusual behavior within ourselves? This is part of what Odin teaches, that you must sometimes act and be someone different than who you normally are. You must make that part of you in order to make real changes in your life. Without these changes, we cannot truly hope to evolve.

Odin travels because he searches, and he searches because he wants to know, to evolve, to change constantly and to make those changes part of that one whole of who he is. He is not always terrifying and destructive, just as well as he is not always understanding and firm. He may not always have the answers, but he does have an understanding of many things in life. He had to be able to reconfigure himself so he would be better suited to a specific situation. These are not aspects, but they are indeed a self. A constant expanding sense of self that has endless potential. He shows us not only how to break our habits, but to understand ourselves at the core. He shows us that in order to change, grow, and evolve as people and spiritual beings, we must first let go of our material things. We must let go of our ego, of who we are in order to gain a new outlook, a new understanding, and a new personality that works with us. The past is not forgotten, and neither are those other parts of ourselves, but he teaches us to interchange between them as we need to so that we can better face the world as it is. There are many ways to evolve, change, and expand yourself. All are valid ways of the self. Odin rips me apart and remakes me as someone else. Yet I am still the same person I was before it happened. I just have new qualities, ideas, and opinions. The All Father is an expanding mind. His mind evolves constantly, and if we wish to know his secrets, his words, his ideals, we must first be able to remove ourselves to make way for his way. Only to otherwise be crushed in the end if we cannot change.

This journey is not easy and there are many challenges ahead for us. We have to be able to change ourselves, we have to be able to see beyond our own veil of reality if we want to look into another persons view of life. To do any kind of spiritual work, we must know at least of some portion of who we are. We can't understand everything about ourselves, not in one lifetime. We can attempt to learn about ourselves, and to accept ourselves for not only who we are, but who we are becoming. That if we can't love ourselves, maybe there is something we need to change or figure out for ourselves so we can achieve self-acceptance.

There are moments when you have to go inside yourself. Moments when you cannot deny there is something wrong inside of you. Sometimes I feel like there is an inner turmoil that I have to deal with from within, but in order to do that I have to cut myself off from everything else in order to achieve any kind of enlightenment. The only way to be happy in some cases, is to simply destroy myself, sacrifice myself to myself. I have to go into myself in order to attain the knowledge and wisdom appropriate to finally come out of the rut I am in. If I do not do this, then it continues to build up until I explode. The inner voice of myself is telling me I have to listen, but it's those little things that we push aside which affects us. I wish there was a better way to go about it, but for me the only way to stop from being sad and depressed is to feel those emotions to the best of my ability to do so. After finding that center and that peace within, I often come out calm and collected than before. I have a greater understanding of why and how I can prevent it the next time.

Odin is a trickster god as well as one who seeks knowledge. There's a great many things he can teach you, but he can also be rather selfish at times. He can work the ways of wyrd and change someones idea, or implant something within you. He has the ability to affect cultures, making himself extremely popular. This ability has the effect of changing someone's perceptions of something specific. It can be about a TV show or a thing you might think is associated with him. If he is ever mentioned in anything through pop-culture, it means that he organized it that way. Odin is a master manipulator with the power to alter minds. There's a reason why people look up to him, there's a reason why people want to be around him. It's because he makes it so.

Working with Odin hasn't been easy, but he has taught me a lot about spirit-working. I have successfully established my own form of tradition because of my working with him. He directs me to tools that I might need for crafting, or even something that I might need to buy for a specific rite. Odin tends to be all about ceremonial rites in different ways. He wants things done in a timely fashion, but also is very understanding about what you can or cannot do. There have been many times that I have asked for clarity about certain things, and over time he made it clear of how I was supposed to perform something. How he made it clear was by directing me to buy specific books, or even requesting a card reading or other divination from someone. He's always made it a habit to look out for me, and help me deal with my personal problems, as well as make sure I am getting the proper guidance in a specific skill set.

I went through a lot of initiations with Odin. The first was a blood sacrifice. The other initiations were mental, and very traumatizing. There was a point I had trouble with myself. In order to do this work properly, you have to dive into aspects of yourself. He would tell me that I would have to deal with myself and like myself if I were to ever achieve anything. This one experience I will never forget. It was when I was forced to return to a place I had all but forgotten. In the past, I visited a temple of many rooms. These rooms seemed to reflect aspects of myself. One of the doors in particular led into a dark chamber. Nothing was in there but darkness, and that is where I locked a portion of myself away. This particular aspect of myself took the shape of a half transformed werewolf. It represented everything negative about myself. The goal of returning to this place was to face it. I had been there a few different times, and I was afraid of what might happen if this wolf were to actually get a hold of me. It would actually run to me, like it was going to attack me. I would shut the door every time and lock it. Odin made me go back and deal with this problem. I let the wolf out, and it ran up to me like it always had. Then it picked me up and devoured me. In this vision, I felt the sharp teeth from its mouth as I traveled down to its throat. It was all disgusting and slimy. I remember feeling dread. It was so surreal! It was as if I were actually being eaten alive! When I felt myself go down into the wolfs stomach, it was like I lifted up. Everything seemed blurry at first, then I could see

96

clearly. I had actually become the creature! I saw my hands as claws with fur down my arms. Everything animal and primal began to disappear, and I had returned to normal. I secluded myself from everyone after that experience and dealt with the one thing I had always felt about myself. I realized I had hated myself for who and what I was. I felt bad for the wolf and bad for myself. I tortured myself. I felt such shame, and such sympathy. Eventually I was able to get over it and return to my everyday life, but it was truly a life changing experience. After that, everything began to set events in motion for me. I felt better about myself, happier and more alive than I had in years. My practice with Odin deepened, and I was finally able to move on from my self-hate.

Since that time, my practice has evolved over and over. The things I offered him were always changing. He seems to be happy with black candles and various acts that involve some form of writing or particular skill. I made my own rune set, as well as my own personal altar which you saw in chapter seven. Odin is associated with darkness in my opinion, and can protect you from entities who may also be lurking within it. If you can't afford a statue of Odin try a journal, ravens, wizard figurines, eyeballs, and wizard hats. Tools can be hallowed (made sacred) in his honor, like swords or knives. Contrary to popular belief, Odin welcomes all people into the religion of heathenry. He isn't picky about who he has working for him. A lot of people seem to be surprised that a gay male would even begin to work with Odin. In the years I have practiced this religion, he has never made mention of my sexuality and doesn't seem to particularly interested if someone is from another culture or skin tone. He sees most humans as equally as anyone else.

Poem to Odin: From the Slain

And From the Depth it came
Walling in pain
A creature ever so fierce
It was darkness
It was fear
None like you ever seen nor hear
And it said take my hand, I will show you the way

So away I went with a little dismay
Only to fall a deep into a cave
It was a place I could be
A place that was just for me

There I lay
So alone, so afraid
But there was a Light Ray
A way to be
I took it and came into being

The power invested in me
I grabbed the shimmering light
Away I flew into the air anew
No more sadness, no more pain
I am the one who has come from being slain

The depths of my heart had killed me, but I had
reached out far and I had reached so much that I
became
ONE
Now I understand the ways in which flow

So I shall teach you if you want to know
But, be weary, this path isn't easy
You may find yourself dealing with something queasy
To go upon this journey with me,
It is to find clarity!

By: Ravenous Nightwind/Theodoric Dukka

Sun. 2/10/2013

A Quote from Me

"Let it all go away from what I know to be true. Just let the pain come through. Let it all be quick and slow. Only because I know that I need to experience it all. Let the knowledge seep in through my skull. Let me know, let me see, let me be beyond what I knew. I want to rise up and scream, let the pain come through me. Let the magic of self be known. Ordeal is a magick most will never know. Experience the pain, the suffering and lose all that you know. Come back out, changed forever more and you'll know again."

Prayer to Odin

"I call to Odin, God of Wisdom and Magic. I thank you Odin for teaching me your ways, bringing me up, and helping me to understand things. Hail to you to Odin All Father!"

"Hail to Odin, wisest of councils. For with his guidance, wisdom, and knowledge, I know that I can

become the best that I know my self to be. For the self and for life. Oh Odin, I honor thee."

Quotes from Odin

"A butterfly cannot become a butterfly unless it faces the harsh colds of winter."

"Magic is part of your senses. These practices of magic are an extension; much like how you smell or taste. It's not about what you can do but about what you can sense. If you can't have faith in it then there is no reason you should be practicing."

"Learning & studying is a long drawn out process. It is not something that can be completed in a month or several months. It will take years. Just because you are a master, does not mean you have learned everything, it just means you have experience."

"Stay focused or you will lose interest. Combine who you are into your practice, then you will find answers."

"You must learn what calls you to learn it despite what anyone says. What you feel drawn to will lead you to who you will become. Do not let others limitations limit you. Only abide by your own restrictions."

"There are many books out there which contain many different perceptions. No one book is the same, though they are similar; each contains a knowledge of *its own. If you wish to learn anything you must first learn what you have learned over again. No one book contains the knowledge of all things and so when you study, you shouldn't bind your self to one simple book. Your studies should have an infinite number of the same type of book to take from. What ever draws you to that specific book is the book you must read if you hope to attain the knowledge you so desire."*

"What you learn, you shall learn again."

Chapter 10

Frigga

A lot of people forget about the small things in life. They forget about what they have, what they own. They don't realize that things could have been turned around for them. Life isn't so easy for everyone. Everyone has a different situation, obligations, and luck. Frigga is a goddess that encompasses a lot of different aspects of life. It isn't just about being at home and doing chores. It's about organization and making things run correctly. As the wife of Odin, Frigga has a lot of responsibilities she has to perform. She has to make sure everyone is taken care of, that the house is in order, or that finances are secure. At the same time, she also governs over wyrd and the luck of people. She can see into the threads of wyrd and access information, or even change the fate of someone. In some stories she is even known to screw around with her own husband, attempting to teach him a lesson. They say that Frigga knows all things that will happen, but does not reveal them. She holds the keys to the secrets of our lives, as well as how we can organize our lives. With her guidance we can develop skills for business, sewing, wyrd working, and household upkeep.

There seems to be some confusion about how Frigga may be similar or even the same as Freya. To me, they will always be separate goddesses. The vibes

I get from them are very different from one another. Frigga works with wyrd in a different way than Freya does. I was taught that wyrd can appear in many forms, and it was Frigga who taught me how wyrd works. Wyrd is a complex web of information and energy. It's vast and encompasses the entirety of everything that is. She said that wyrd is like a tapestry. Everyone has their own, but they are linked to the larger tapestry that is all. This tapestry can be read in different ways, and typically may reveal itself through some form of symbology. Frigga almost never goes into specific detail, but she has told me before that they as deities are not all powerful beings. They have limits and they can only influence things to a certain degree depending on the situation and circumstance. She says that no one can see all there is to see, not even herself. Everything about Frigg is about getting things done or allowing yourself to stop and think about everything, connecting yourself to the forces in which lay around you all the time but go unnoticed. She teaches me how to tap into these powers by "listening"

I always thank Frigga for my home, family, friends, relationship, finances, and my overall life. She has helped me to organize my life as a way of understanding what I need to do. With organization comes order and schedules. It may seem like a big mess of frustration, but in reality it can be the best thing for us. On the other hand, she can work things out in a way where something happens for the good of someone, or for the worse. Her skills with wyrd are immense and are not something to be taken lightly. Anyone who manages to piss her off would soon regret it. Just because she's associated with the household, does not mean she is weak or disconnected with protecting herself, or showing you about respect.

Frigga is very concerned about me just living my life. Her and I do not have many boundaries. She often likes to check on things for me by looking in on a certain situation. She's always said that I should just be happy, to live my life and not worry about things. She likes it when I dedicate specific tasks to her, like cleaning and making things. The biggest thing she has taught me is: how to be thankful for the little things that I have, for the things that many often take for granted. She helps you to relax and live your life, but at the same time lets you know that things have to be taken care of. To go to Frigga as thanks in humility shows that you are thankful for your life. Look at everything that you have instead of wanting something you don't have. We forget these simple things and fail to realize that it could of just as easily been turned around. I have found true quality of life when I work with Frigga. It isn't what you want or what you think might be good for you, it's what you already have that matters the most. Having a shower, clothing, money, friends, family, etc. All of it is what we might have, something that someone else may not have. Instead of searching for more, we should look at what is already available to us instead. To be thankful for everything, especially the simple things. All this composes into a sense of humility about the self, and about ones life.

Prayers to Frigga

"I call to Frigga, Goddess of household and wyrd. I thank you Frigga for my friends, family, relationship, home, finances, and life. Hail to you Frigga!"

"Hail to Frigga, Wyrd keeper. With her guidance, stability, and sight. I know I will become the best that I know my self to be. For weaving my fate according to what I know is right inside my heart."

"Frigga, Help me to be thankful for everything I have. Help me to be organized, help me to take care of myself and those I provide for. Hail to you Frigga, All Mother, Lady of Asgard.

Quotes from Frigga

"You must first understand that all things are uncertain, when you know that, you will know things you can't understand."

"Smoke is like energy, it moves around. We need only tap into energy to understand."

Chapter 11

Skadhi

Skadhi was one of the first goddesses I started working with. She is very much against people not standing up for themselves. She doesn't like bullies, and she prefers that you not cower away from confrontations if it's something you absolutely need to do. I had a lot of family problems when I started my work with her. My mom..well, let's just say that she had a tendency to take out her problems on me in an emotional and verbal way. Skadhi wasn't having any of that! She told me that I should stand up for myself and I shouldn't put up with anyone's crap. I had a serious change at that time and it was something a lot of people didn't like because I began to be extremely honest with people.

There would be nights where I would sit at my altar and cry about what someone said or did to me. I wasn't sure how to speak to people or how to handle a situation. Skadhi brought me up from all of that confusion and self-pity. She made me see that the only way people would stop picking on me is if I showed them I am not to be messed with. That if someone does mess with me, then I have every right to protect myself. Sure enough, people had a lot of disputes about things. It came to the point where I began to be to serious with people. I started to have this attitude that I didn't like about myself. Dare I say, I was beginning to sound more like Skadhi and possess traits similar to hers. If you don't know what that's like, it's cold and hard as stone. I had to check myself because her influence was very strong. I had to embrace it in the beginning in order to get past all my problems. I didn't see this as an excuse to treat people like crap though, that was never my intention. Although it seems no matter what you say, people will always find something to nitpick at because they aren't happy with your attitude.

Skadhi taught me so much about self-respect. Everyone has worth, no matter who they are or what they did. Everyone is worth something and nobody should be treated unfairly or poorly just because they're different or unusual. Everyone has their own unique qualities. She wants you to be wild and free. At the same time, she doesn't want you to let people to walk all over you. When you work with her, you have to find a balance between saying something, and not. I would find that she would get angry or upset with me if I didn't follow through with her instructions to the letter.

Sometimes you have to explain why you can't tell someone off. Gods and Goddesses don't live by our social standards. I had to establish some ground rules with her a little bit because there are just certain things we shouldn't say or do in today's society. She understood everything I said and was very reasonable about it in her own way. She still wanted me to show no mercy towards people who were trying to suppress me or hurt me. She seemed like she cared about me in her own cold jotun way. It's not the same thing as a loving goddess. Skadhi is very silent when she doesn't have anything to say. She doesn't give people hugs or make you feel loved. Instead, Skadhi gives you this overall cold and hard feeling like no other deity I have encountered.

If Skadhi taught me anything, it's how to be faithful to yourself and when you shouldn't put up with other people. She taught me self-respect and honor for myself. Skadhi isn't just all about winter and hunting. As cold and harsh as she is, she cares in her own way. Her way is being cold and harsh to people. Her love doesn't feel warm and cozy, it feels cold and distant. That is who she is, and how she comes off to me. If she didn't care, she wouldn't make an effort to teach me anything.

She has the abilities of an experienced tracker and can transform herself into a raging snowstorm. She can teach you the ways of archery and hunting, as well as surviving the cold. She has knowledge about the stars and may teach it to those who are willing to put in the effort to learn. She doesn't like it when people are lazy, wanting her to do all the work. She is a no nonsense type of individual and will not work with people who intentionally bully others.

A lot of my work with her revolves around nature spirits, particularly those similar to herself. She introduced me once to three wind wights whom I am now great friends with and give offerings to every Saturday. She seems to be mostly connected with wights of sky and weather. However, she's also connected to wolves, bears, and other trees and animals that surround the mountains. I feel her presence is the strongest in winter. She has helped me to develop a sense of thick skin and adapt myself to every situation that I come across. She isn't gentle when it comes to learning about things. If you can't learn it as she teaches it, then she may eventually just leave, especially if you don't want to take the time to even consider the lessons she's offering. The advice she gives is very harsh and at times, disconcerting. She makes it a habit to be blunt, honest, and extremely straightforward. When she doesn't like something, she'll let you know. She doesn't play games or mess with your head. She hates excuses most of all, and doesn't tolerate people making silly excuses for not wanting to do something. Especially if it concerns sticking up for yourself or doing something she specifically asked you to do. She's really big about truth and despises lies. If you lie to her, she will most certainly find out and take her revenge out on you in some way. She prefers the harsh truth over anything else.

My offerings for Skadhi are mostly candles and scents. She's very partial to the sugar cookie scent oil I picked up at the store. Most Jotunar seem to be into sweets more than any other food from what I have heard and experienced. I give her white or grey candles because of her association with mountains and snow.

Quotes from Skadhi

"You must understand that the truth will not change others for who they are. The mountain will not bend to truth or the trees to uproot themselves to it. The truth is your own, but do not let others take it from you and do not let it taint or corrupt others to convert"

"Be fierce as the wind & mountains tumbling down. Be the purest form of yourself & don't hold back. Keep the balance within you & never be held down."

Prayers to Skathi

"Hail to Skadhi, Huntress of the Wilds. With her guidance, fierceness, & cunning willing heart. I know I will be the best I know my self to be. For to speak the truth in honor of the self, to never let anyone get me down or stop me from doing what I know to be truth. Oh Skadhi, I honor thee.

"I call to Skathi, Fierce Huntress, Winter Goddess. I thank you for teaching me how to be as strong as stone, fierce as wind, and harsh as snow! Hail to you Skathi, Fierce Huntress."

"Skadhi, help me to be strong and stand up for myself. Help me to be honest, blunt, and true. Guide me in your ways and help me to stand on my own!"

A Poem: Winter Ends Spring Begins

I stand at the edge of winter
I look out at the snowy blanket
Across far which I can see
The coldest breath of winter blows out to make its last mark on the land
I seek to appreciate the glory of winter

To the Goddess Skathi,
Maid of the winter glade
I seek to uphold her quick fast wits
Her intuition that she will come out victorious

Even if Idunna brings her spring rejuvenation of life

Skathi will yet return again
Winter is the time for seclusion and isolation
The time which we think about what we want to bring
in our lives
The darkest of things are here
The secrets of all thought of

We are in the between times
For spring is coming and we need it here
The trees are beginning to wake
Snow will lift from the ground
Nature will create
Green will sprout from the plants abound

I can hear its horn,
Its sound
The trees are singing
Life is gleaming
Though in winters embrace,
Life awaits
Soon I shall step once again into the grass
The sun will be bright again at last
So hear me now I say,
Spring is on its way

This poem was inspired by the coming of spring and my appreciation of winter and the overall process of the changing of seasons. It's not only a devotional poem towards Skathi, but also for Idunna. Thank Skathi and everything she has taught me, I thank her for being there with your cold heart and stone demeanor. Without her, I could not be the person I am today! Hail to Skathi, the glorious Winter Queen!

Chapter 12

Freyr

Freyr has a very joyful demeanor and can be quite fun to hang around. He does possess a serious side which is often very mysterious in some ways. He expects a certain level of gratitude and also wants me to be aware of what I'm eating. To understand that all things are living, even rocks, trees, birds, etc. He says that nature is the pathway into the spiritual world. His path is long and rough to understand. My original quest in seeking out Freyr was to glean his understanding of animals. However, Freyr had other ideas. My first lessons with Freyr were about plants, learning their languages. He would constantly talk about plants and how he wanted me to be involved with them. This wasn't my original plan and at first, I refused. Over time I began to accept the fact that me working with animal spirits wasn't going to happen, not through him anyway.

He brought me to a place in trance. Usually it was a place of forest and green. Sometimes he would appear as a giant person with leather armor and other times he would appear as a young boy. When he began my training with plants, it was all about connectivity. He looked dirty to me. He was covered in black and brown dirt. He was tall, giant size, and held out his hand. When he opened it he revealed a seed. He told me that the seed would help me to understand plants, to help them grow and prosper. Then he shoved the seed into my chest. It actually hurt, the act of doing this. I felt it in a physical way, but once inside, itwas gentle. I felt its vines moving about inside my body, creating a sort of spiritual tattoo of vines on my spiritual body.

At first I shrugged it all off. "No, this isn't happening. I just imagined it." I would tell myself. Then over time I noticed that plants grew better, and even animals like bees and butterflies would often come up to me suddenly. I started to see the differences in the reactions to certain plants. The plants would grow better for me and sprout early. Some plants more than others. The ones who favored me would often get fairly large.

Eventually it all led to planting a garden and tending to it, but also allowing that piece of land to remain mostly untouched by human hands. I now have a well established boarder to prevent it from being ran over by a mower. I plant new plants in it every spring. I also grow plants from seeds as well as buy established plants at the store.

Freyr always talks about connectivity and how nature is everywhere. Even in the cracks of the street you can see nature. Just because you live in the city doesn't mean it is completely devoid of nature. Nature is everywhere, within us and around us. No matter where we go, we will always find nature. In big cities nature are the trees, the birds, the vines growing on the side of buildings. We are also nature, we are human animals. We are mammals and co-exist with many different creatures of different species.

Working with Freyr has been more about cultivation and gardening than anything else. I'm sure people look at that and go "well that's easy". You have no idea! There's a lot of digging involved, buying specific plants to bring in certain types of insects, and then actually understanding the plant spirits themselves and what they want.

Freyr has helped me grasp the basics of reviving the tradition of working with spirits around the home. It is in no way an easy or glamorous job. It is however very rewarding as much as it is backbreaking. It requires effort and respect towards the plants you might be killing. It requires hard work. It isn't just all spiritual woo stuff. It's also about digging up the dirt and transplanting the plants who called out to you and then caring for them in the best way you possibly can. Working with Freyr is not an easy job, because it mostly requires these things and more.

One of the lessons of Freyr is to enjoy life. To see the natural world in all its beauty and danger. Even if that means you're in the city in an apartment. Look at the plants growing in the cracks or the trees near by. Look at the urban animals around you. It's to see and enjoy life and everything around you. That abundance is around us no matter where we go. He taught me that plants have their own language and that we can speak to them if we give ourselves time to adjust to them. Plants can be hard to understand, but he helped me figure out how to communicate with them spiritually, by telling me to listen, but not to expect words. Plants speak through energies, this is the lesson he wished to teach me so that I too could work with plants and become allies with them.

Part of my spiritual work is in the garden. Physically talking to plants and tending to their needs, even if it's only observing. It's back breaking and leaves you full of sweat and heat. You leave the garden and come inside to rest and feel completely empty, nothing left but your breathing and hard beating heart. Especially if you happen to be transplanting already established plants into a new area because they aren't getting enough sunlight. Working with deities of the land is not easy work, and neither is farming. You might think it's easy because you're working with spirits and gods who are stuck in the ground and cannot move, but when you attempt to move the soil, it does not move so easily. The soil can be rough and hard. So we too must be rough in life if we need to be. The garden can teach you many things. The spirits of the wild will show you if you are willing to learn.

Just because something is small and seemingly insignificant, it doesn't mean that it's worthless. It doesn't mean that it can't grow into something more. This is the wisdom that plants offer. Seeds are small, a lot like our dreams, our desires, but when we nurture them by doing the things we need to do in order to make it happen, we make our dreams come true and turn our seeds into giant forests. If I have learned anything, plants and Freyr have taught me that nothing is insignificant. Everything is beautiful and can always become more than what it appears to be. It's being able to see the potential in everything and everyone!

The one thing about plants is that their energy is silent, not weak but just not always apparent. Unless they want it to be. I feel like the more I work with them spiritually, the more I will come to understand who they are as individuals. What they want and what they need is important to me, it isn't just about what I can get from them. It's also about the environment and what the wild needs. It's a powerful learning process that makes you see more than yourself, but also the entirety of the place you live. You start to see others needs, their views. Not the limited human view, but rather that all life has a need, a want, a yearning for something. If it's a bee buzzing around for nectar and pollen, or it's a plant growing for sunlight so it can live. The point of life, the purpose every living thing strives for, is to live!

I try to connect myself to each plant that I transplant or sow. I want to let the plant know I wish to work with them. Even if they don't, then they know I mean them no harm and want to be their friend if they ever feel ready for it. I like using herbs for my practice and they are part of it to some degree, but working with them also should be something on a personal level too. Such as growing them and tending to them and even respecting them as individual beings. It means asking them if I can cut off a limb and use them for spiritual or magical purposes. If that answer is no then I leave them alone! I try to respect them as individuals, people with feelings of their own.

Just because someone works with a Vanir god or goddess doesn't mean that we get taken down a road that is easy. Like every experience that involves a deity, it is different and difficult based on how they choose to interact with us. If you think that planting crops and tending to plants is easy, you have another thing coming. It's hard work, work that blisters your fingers. That's why they use tractors in the fields! Working with Freyr I have found certain things that can be difficult to understand. Freyr talks about how to sense and feel plants, and how to connect ones self to the earth. These things require a form of specialized training. You don't just get the ability over night, you have to work at it. My offerings to Freyr often consist of green or brown candles, an earthy scent, or my own personal energy. I also work in the garden in his honor.

Quotes from Freyr

"Not every experience will be the same. No one will approach you in the exact same way as another. When you journey into nature, it will be different."

"The plants & the animals can be hard to understand, but if you watch & and pay attention then you can achieve a better understanding. After all, what you read in books can only take you so far, but to experience it is to give you a deeper understanding."

Prayer to Freyr

"I call to Freyr, and I thank you Freyr for teaching about plants and their languages, for teaching me how to comune with the earth. Hail to you Freyr, God of Fields and Forest!"

"Freyr, help me to understand the language of the wild. Work with me so that I can work with animals and plants. Allow me to understand their wants and needs. Not for myself, but for their benefit, so that I can help create an environment suitable for them in this seemingly modern world."

Chapter 13

Thor

Thor is a god whom has always helped me deal with things concerning will and strength. He didn't make it easy for me. A lot of people have stories about Thor helping them and making them feel strong. I'm not sure what that involves, but it felt very different for me. He would tell me that I can deal with things, but he wouldn't just take my pain away. He said that I am stronger than I know myself to be, and I can achieve things if I put my will and effort into it. He didn't take away my problems, he made me deal with my emotional issues and situations. He made me stronger by telling me that I am strong, and that you just have to find that strength in yourself if you want to truly get past something.

He was there for me in a time of great stress and pain. Often times he would make his presence known to me in different ways. Usually it was through just feeling he was there. He was always standing beside me in some way, making me feel like it was okay, watching over me. You know the kind of person who's just there for you but they only stand there and watch you do things even if you fail? That's the kind of person Thor is. If I failed he would tell me to get back up again and keep trying. He would say that strength isn't inside your muscles, it's inside yourself, a mental and emotional thing. He didn't seem to look down on me for crying or being upset. If you want to do anything in life, you have to work for it. You can't just sit around and expect things to change when you're not doing anything to make it better. Even if it isn't getting any better, you can't just give up. No matter how dirty it gets, you just have to keep going through the mud until you reach where you need to be

Thor is not exactly the most emotional person, but he does tend to be very gentle to people in understanding their feelings. I would say he's one of the few who truly get down in peoples problems in a personal way. He's not one of those gods who are to serious or expect glamorous things from you. He told me once before he didn't expect huge rites from me, that ceremonies and all that were not his thing. He said all I had to give him was my honor and respect by just calling to him every Thursday. He didn't want it to be a huge ritual or practice, he wanted it to be casual. He didn't have any specifications to what he wanted as long as I did something for him.

When I think about my relationship with Thor, I think about how he was a big brother to me. He was there for me when everyone else wasn't. He didn't do things at a distance. He made his presence known to me in a blunt way. Most of the time, he did nothing for me. All he really did was just stand there and watch me fail or succeed. He would offer his advice of how I might better my situation or how I should handle it, but he didn't fix everything for me. He left everything up to me.

Offerings for Thor would often be my own energy, or perhaps a candle I made for him if I was asking something specific of him. Thor can be called upon for house blessings, or to hallow specific places.

He'll even come in and clear the space out if you're willing to help. I don't offer food or drinks to him because of my limited budget. Instead, it's candles, personal energy, or even a scent he likes. I've found that Thor likes cinnamon roll scent.

Thor would much rather sit around and talk to people as a group. He is one of those gods who would sit down casually with his hammer and eat pizza while watching a brawl, playing fantasy games, or Elder Scrolls. Yes, video games are part of my UPG with him, and there was actually a time I would play a game for him. Thor is literally a bro kinda guy that you can just sit and chill with to have fun. Thor is a jolly man with a very good sense of humor. He's the kind of god who would do crazy things just because. If you dared him to go skinny dipping, you'd probably be paying up because I bet he would do it. He's up for any of our modern challenges. He doesn't speak in cryptic messages and tends to be very direct and blunt about everything. He is harsh but he proves a point that you can't always rely on someone else, you sometimes have to rely on yourself but know when to bring others in. With Thor, it's not about striking fast and hard, it's about showing courage and strength. Not only in the face of adversity, but to rise it up in yourself and obtain the inner strength that you'll need to deal with a problem.

Without Thor, I could not be where I am today! I would still be down, into myself. I couldn't think of a more proper way to thank him than by dedicating this to him. He'll always be a brother to me. He'll always mean the world to me. For everything he has done for me, for everything he helped me to achieve and understand about myself and others. Thank you so much Thor..for everything!

Quotes from Thor

"Real strength is found within the spirit inside you."

"Strength is not in the arms, feet, or mind, but what is in the heart. Right and wrong is subjective, but there is a general understanding that all people abide by. Strength comes from within and you need only seize the courage to pull it out and to do what you feel is right."

"The biggest thing you can do for yourself is making your own choices. Live for yourself & take care of yourself. Help those you find worthy when you feel the time is right."

"You must do what you feel is right & uphold yourself as well as others you might find worthy. Only uphold what you can bear, but not false promises."

Prayers to Thor

"I call to Thor, God of Storms. I thank you Thor for helping me to realize where strength comes from and how to raise it up within myself, to wield my own hammer. Thank you for your wisdom and guiding me and being there for me. Hail to Thor!"

"Thor, help me to raise my hands against those who would wish to harm me. Help me protect those

who are under my care. Teach me how to raise my own
hammer and wield my own power."

Chapter 14

Loki

Loki is the God of change. He's helped me through a lot of things. He's helped me deal with my anxiety, my fears. He's helped me deal with other people. When others saw only a weird person or a monster, Loki saw potential and understood me when no one else did. Many consider him to be a god of chaos, but to me he will always be the godly father of change. He took his time to understand me for who I am. He helped me deal with life and my personal issues.

Loki tends to use different methods of interaction with people. The most common method from what I have seen, is making people feel uncomfortable in some way. He sends them odd visions, or makes them feel uneasy when he makes his presence known. It seems to be his signature for some reason. I've seen it a lot with people who are new to working with him. It's like he's testing the waters. I've had people tell me the same thing I went through before. That he made them feel strange, or that he suddenly popped into their head and they saw weird, disgusting, or disturbing things when before, they had no reason to think of him. For whatever reason he chooses to do this, I feel that there must be some kind of personal test he wants us to go through. Each of us may see something different or feel something different, but the similarity is that he makes us feel uncomfortable in one way or another through mental meddling.

Loki was probably the god that I feared the most. It was mainly due to his reputation. When he came into my life, he made himself known in different ways. He would respect my wishes of not wanting to work with him. Even though I said no, he would return months later each time. He would make me feel scared. He would make me fear him. It made me really uncomfortable. I knew it was on purpose. He wanted to teach me that just because it feels weird, doesn't mean it's a bad thing. He taught me a lot about accepting my fears and anxieties as part of myself. He taught me how to see and feel around me through energy. He's been very kind to me. He makes me feel accepted and understood. He taught me how to accept my fears and move on. To look into the past for guidance and see my own faults, but to only look for wisdom. Not to get caught up in what happened. He has helped me to change my life in such a way that my anxiety doesn't affect me in the same way as it did before. Even if I have issues, he always seems to remind me that all I have to do is look within. To look at what I have been through and attempt to learn from it. He's helped me to better my life and myself to a degree that I never thought was possible.

He said to focus on myself, all my fears and anxieties. He told me to feel them and see them. To partially relive those moments and accept them and myself as me. He took me inside myself. He made love to myself, and absorb all the things that were negative. He told me that I must accept it all, and that when things happen, I must accept it and take it within me.

He said there was no reason to be afraid because I could get past this. I just had to love and accept myself before I could move on or love anyone else. If there is one thing I will always remember, it is the fact that everyone has their own thoughts and opinions. As much as I love to express my own, I have to accept that other people won't believe or like it. Not everyone is open to change or seeing things in a different way. Which is something else I must also keep in mind when I voice my own concerns and experiences. That's something Loki has taught me, always be aware that change is there and that it happens. Not everyone will be willing to accept it or understand it in the same way that I do. I can't change people or make them see things that they don't want to see.

He will appear to me with a slender but elegant form, wearing a old style Victorian suit with black hair combed back. He has high cheek bones and a even forehead with a long face and long nose, (he looks nothing like Tom Hiddleson) with a dashing appearance. He often gives me a smirk that makes me worry. His words are sharp and clever. He often speaks to me about fears and anxieties. He has made it possible for me to transform myself and my fears into something more useful. He's told me that it doesn't matter what people think because they don't know who I am. Their judgment does not truly matter. Instead, I should take that judgment and learn from it and adapt to it if there is a reason to. His most famous words that I remember are "When you let go of fear, you can do anything." I often use those words to help me cope with my own fears and worries that often plague me in everyday life. I refer to him as The God of Change because he takes many forms and can alter life circumstances from something simple or from something complicated. Loki understands change and that it is needed. He can help us to adapt to specific situations that might otherwise stress us out. He would often come to me, making me feel odd. This was his way of showing me that I can face those feelings and transform them. He can teach me how to change and adapt if I choose it. Unlike other deities, Loki seems very understanding of those who are different, of those who have mental conditions or physical disabilities. He doesn't tell me to push away those things, but instead to see the realization in my fears and worries and learn to think logically and more productively. Even if you say no to Loki in a polite way, he will still return later. He will plague your mind. Not in a stressful way, but in a way that makes things remind you of him. He will work with you and sometimes play with you, but laugh at you when you fuck up. He can be as kind and gentle as he sees fit, but he can also be hard and fiery.

He is change itself, and he makes you see things from a different perspective. He can help us become better people if we strive to see the truth in his words and actions. He can help us change and evolve just as he does. This isn't a bad thing. Change is good, but a lot of people are afraid of it. Sometimes it takes negative experiences to make things better. They don't want to go through that ordeal. In the end, everyone has to change if they wish to improve themselves in their faults. Offerings for Loki are usually orange candles or anything spicy. He seems to be really fond of cinnamon scents. I often associate the color orange with Loki because it's a color of fear and anxiety for me.

"Fear, anxiety, become part of me so that I can master it, so that I can master myself. To know myself. Let that make me become stronger! For fear is part of everyone, but the best types of fear are the ones that allow you to evolve!"
-- Theodoric Dukka

Loki's Lesson: Dealing with Fears & Anxiety

Find a place where you will not be disturbed for at least ten minutes. Sit there in the dark and breathe in for four and hold, then breathe out and hold for four. Repeat this process over and over. Allow yourself to drift inwardly into a meditation. Around you, imagine swirls and ribbons of orange light. Orange is the color of change, of fear and anxiety. Allow them to surround you, and within that orange light, see what you're afraid of. See your anxieties and fears as they were when you experienced them. Loki says that these are part of yourself, so we must learn to accept ourselves without pushing those emotions away. In this we gain the knowledge of ourselves and how to best deal with our own problems. When you watch the replaying of these events, imagine that the ribbons they are in, to enter your stomach. Now let another scene come in, see it as it is, remember how you felt. Absorb it into yourself again and again. It's okay to cry, to feel uneasy. This is normal.

Once you have felt that it's enough, imagine those swirling orange ribbons of light in your stomach to then spread throughout your entire body. Allow yourself to accept those feelings because that is you, and it is beautiful because it is yourself. Allow yourself to come to terms with what has happened to you and understand that it's okay, understand that you can only be yourself and no one else, that it is never wrong to feel those things.

Remember my quote from Loki: "When you remove fear, you can do anything." Removing your fear doesn't mean you push it away, it means you accept it as part of your being. Once you face those fears, you can overcome them and rise above them. You will always have things in life you are afraid of, but that doesn't mean we have to be slave to those feelings. We can make them part of ourselves and move on instead of living in fear. In the end, trust that Loki will guide you out of those fears and anxiety. Trust that he accepts you as you are. For you are not a monster or a weak person. You are yourself, and that is perfection, that is beauty.

Quotes from Loki

"When you let go of fear, you can do anything."

"You must learn to adapt and use that adaptation."

"Learn how to change, but know how to stay the same. This is an ability that few can claim."

"I call to Loki, God of Change. I thank you Loki for teaching me, helping me deal with my problems and helping me to adapt to situations and learning my faults so that I may become a better person. Thank you for guiding me. Hail to Loki!"

"Loki, help me to deal with my anxieties and fears. Show me how to deal with myself. Others see only a nobody, a monster. Bring me the wisdom to understand myself, to understand my fears and anxieties. Help me to see my own potential so that I can raise myself up from this pit and live my life to the fullest!"

Chapter 15

Freya

She began working with me when I wanted help in divination. I had always been drawn to crystal balls and cards. I ended up buying a statue of her and she helped me connect to crystals. My first introduction into serious practice with divination was interesting. She had me buy a large crystal ball. When I started my work with it, the crystal began to resonate its own life force. I found out that it was actually connected to a much larger spirit. In the visions I received from viewing in the crystal, this spirit was a huge cavern. I believe this spirit was gender-less, but chose to interact with me in a male voice. They told me that I could call them the Crystal Father. They told me when I needed anything concerning crystal gazing, I could call upon them for guidance. It was a very interesting experience to say the least.

After my initial practice with crystal gazing, Freya wanted to get me involved with cards. Yes, runes were a big thing for me before cards, and they are more Norse in origin. She had other ideas though. She said that I had to be skilled in various things for different people. Just because you learn a divination thing, doesn't mean it will work for everyone. It's good to make or buy various tools for various people. I told her I had concerns. I had a very hard time working with tarot because I couldn't relate to the cards. I would often get interesting vibes off of tarot. But when I went to actually work with them, they wouldn't respond to me like I wanted. I then discovered oracle cards and their unique styles of variety. Freya guided me to card sets so she could help me learn about them. She said I shouldn't worry about things not working, because she was going to teach me how. After a considerable amount of time, I discovered that what she said had come to pass. I had begun to understand various oracle decks. I started using them to dive into my own wyrd. I practiced every Monday, the day which was now designated towards Freya. Everyday I would perform a spread. Detailed spreads were very complicated and often were a review of things. One card drawings ended up being a specific question. After a while, she helped me to develop my own card spread based on the World Tree. Every card was based off one of the nine worlds and were associated with specific things. Things like family, friendships, problems, stress, etc. There was not an ending result in this spread like there was in most card spreads. It simply gave advice about certain things and how someone could handle certain situations.

Freya wasn't just all about divination though. She helped me realize that I am important. She helped me to see my self worth. She said that I am worth something. She said I should love myself and treat myself fairly. There was no shame in crying or being emotional. When things seemed to not work for me, she would reassure me that I would learn in time. It wasn't something that would just come along over night. She was very respectful and honest. She was also very stern, but compassionate. She wasn't like the other deities I work with, whom were all about business as usual. She was a teacher, but she saw things inside of me and helped me to understand myself. Her job as my teacher would often bleed into being my friend. She didn't just let me get away with things though. She was strict and straightforward. She would be blunt with me and tell me exactly what I needed to do. She explained everything in a way that I could understand it, instead of giving me some kind of riddle to solve. She felt that if I was going to practice anything, I would need to know how. The way she comes off to me is sometimes like a caring school teacher, and other times she's like a psychiatrist. It isn't the same as everyone might think of though. She was more understanding and guided me down the path with a firm but sincere tone.

My experience with her was also about diving into wyrd. Wyrd as most of you probably know, is actually someone's personal destiny. That's how I would describe it anyway. Often times, what a person has done or what someone from their past has done, has influenced their life in some way. In some cases, the choices of a family member or even a past life can affect someones wyrd. Wyrd is a complex form of energy that surrounds everyone. It's part of everything we do and are in life. It is incorporated with our luck, our finances, where we work, what opportunities we have, and just essentially everything in life that we experience. By concentrating and using cards, runes, or various other divination methods, we can help people to find clarity in their lives. We can offer advice about how to fix a particular problem or tell them what caused it. Wyrd will often appear to me as strands of purple light. They often appear as rings around an individual and lead to other people, objects, things, and events. Wyrd also connects spirits and deities to a person. Wyrd can even be affected by the spirits or gods you work with. Sometimes, those entities can even change things for you. I only really see the strands of wyrd when I go into trance. The type of trance I enter when I am divining is very different than the trance I use for journeying. When I divine for people, I may use cards or runes. Depending on what card deck I am using, or if I am using runes, responses are different. The cards and runes have spirits associated with them. They tell me what they know when I enter a light trance. Usually what happens in this kind of situation is: I tell the client what the cards or runes say. When I dive in, it's like a plethora of information that surges through me. I may not even remember what was said after the initial reading. Which is why I keep a record of all my readings in a journal. The information that I get often sounds like another person. I am often told by people that I do not sound like myself when I am divining.

I'm not exactly sure where people get the idea that Freya is a female only type of goddess. She can definitely help you to discover your feminine side, but she is much more than just a Lady as her name means. She is a very complex individual with desires and agendas of her own. She's very fond of fruits, art, music, and all manner of different talents. She loves it when people express themselves. She expects the same amount of honesty as she gives to you. She's also quite scary if you get her angry. A lot of people deal with the witchy side of her. She's very fun loving however, and extremely accepting. She is a mistress of magic and a wonderful friend. It seems she's also very interested in soul collection. She alerts people to things, like if a person has a problem with the All Father and they don't know about it, Freya may actually take it upon herself to swoop them up and protect them. I think she likes pissing Odin off to tell you the truth. He knows that she is extremely powerful, that's why she gets away with things. She can be just as scheming and tricky as he can, but she uses different methods that seem to be more honest and up front. She isn't extremely aggressive, but she can definitely pack a punch when she deems it necessary. Freya has this way about her about being free from restrictions. Freyja doesn't always care about rules unless she happens to put them down herself. She is more carefree about her way of practice, but still directs in certain ways. Freya is a goddess that is most associated with Seidr. Freya's magic is often times used to seek out things in some form or another. I get this feeling that Freya has the ability to see through cats eyes. In other words, whatever cats can see, she can also see by either possessing them or tuning herself to them some how. When I look at a cat, I think of her, especially house cats. I think they're her spies.

Working with Freya has been an absolute pleasure. I will often give her fruity scents for offerings. She is very fond of the color red or burgundy. She likes other colors too, like gold, white, blue, purple, and several others. I will often make her burgundy colored candles. Like most other deities, I also offer a portion of my own energy to her. I thank her for everything she has taught me. From divination, to loving myself, and teaching me how to read wyrd, etc.

Prayer to Freya

"I call to Freya, Goddess of Seidr. I thank you for teaching me how to gaze into crystals, read the cards, peer into wyrd, and love myself. Hail to you Freya, Goddess of Seidr!"

"Freya, help me to understand the ways of Seidr. Allow me to look beyond the veil into wyrd. Teach me your ways. Teach me how to read cards, gaze into crystals, to see signs around me, and to see with eyes unclouded. Help me dive into Seidr and the way of trance. Show me the way!"

Chapter 16

Hela

Hela is often depicted to be half living and half dead. She resides in Helheim, at the very bottom of Yggdrasil. My first encounters with Hela were actually a few years before my initial working with her. She first appeared to me as a little girl in a big white nothingness. She had blond hair that was almost white. Her hair was so long it covered her entire face. There was a flash, and her skeletal side was revealed. It had been few years after that meeting that I began to work with her. Before the initial working, I would often pray to her to take souls of dead animals. These animals were often roadkill. I would call upon her when I was driving down the road and ask her to take them in.

In my first working with Hela, she taught me about the dead and decay. She said a part of me had to be like them. She initiated me by asking me to do weird things. She wanted me to put my hand in fire, told me I wouldn't get burnt. I didn't, mainly because I did it quick enough. She wanted me to take the burnt sooty skin and wipe it on my face. I'm still not sure of the purpose for this but, it was part of the transition. The other part was seeing myself long since dead. She said I had to see myself die in the ground before she would allow me to work with her. She sent me images, weird and morbid things that made me uncomfortable. I felt my body drift away into nothing as time passed. I sort of ended up in a peaceful place at that point. After the overall acceptance of what had happened, she took me to her realm. There she sat with me, and we spoke about the terms of working with her. She said that I had to drink from a cup in Helheim. She said that it would be the moment when I would be able to work with her, basically sealing some kind of strange divine deal. She didn't really say anything about the terms of this deal. She only said I had to drink from the cup if I were to work with her. I did end up drinking this it, and it began our initial contract together. Ever since then, I can feel various things about particular plants, animals, and sometimes people. It's like the death, or even the dead sense. It's not a type of feeling that I feel everyday or even at all. There are times I don't notice anything. Whatever it is, it has something to do with Hela. She did something to me that I can't remember. It's sort of like a memory she plucked out of me when I was there in Helheim.

Helheim itself isn't always dark and dank. I think a lot of people see it as a cavern or maybe an underground world. That's not what I saw at all. Helheim actually appeared to me as a vast field, with sunlight, trees, and lush grass. Certain parts of Helheim are pretty dark and eerie, but those are the parts the living aren't supposed to go. Those areas are usually where dark shadows dwell. I'm not sure if they are our worst nightmares brought to life, or if they are other things that deal with part of her power. I was only able to go to Helheim because she allowed me to go. It is actually a very dangerous place if you aren't being guided in. Often times, people aren't even allowed in there.

Hela safeguards the dead against anyone who

might bother them. She makes sure that they're taken care of. Only through her power was I able to connect to the dead. My original reason for working with her was because of my interest in my own family line. She had other ideas though. Instead, she connected me to certain peoples family lines. I have a client who I performed a reading for once. His grandmother actually came into the reading. He told me after everything I said, he knew it was her that was speaking through me. He said only she would ever say the things I told him. He got really emotional about it and said it was weird. He told me he had been thinking about her a lot before the reading, and that it just confirmed she was there watching out for him. I don't typically have to many experiences like this for some reason. I think it has to do with signal clarity, or maybe the dead just don't want to talk. Either way it was really interesting.

Hela's job is to collect souls. She will actually seek out people whom have been abandoned by their gods. She can see into the dark mists of wyrd. She decides when to intervene with someone's life and when not to. She's very blunt, and doesn't care if what she says hurts you. Her words are always the cold hard truth. If she ever tells you to do something, do it. She has the power to make things happen if you don't abide by what she says. Often times she can make someones life miserable until they decide to make it stop. The things she wants people to do often relates to their life. Changes in which someone should do something about, but doesn't want to for whatever reasons they may have. She has the ability to find out hidden secrets about anyone. Hela doesn't play games with people. She's usually very serious, well composed, and very calm. She tends to be very slow at walking, but she's amazingly quick when she's angry. Hela is a dark goddess, and not in the sense of being bad or evil. She rules over certain powers of darkness. She can command diseases and illnesses, they are her minions. There is a good reason why Odin fears her, and it's because of her power over death that scares him. He has great respect for her but wasn't exactly pleased that I began working with her. If Hela can make Odin afraid, you know there's something more to her than meets the eye.

I associate Hela with skeleton keys because of her ability to find out secrets. She can unlock inner doors for people. She will have you go through a series of trials to better your life. It seems like she wants to help the living as much as she wants to help the dead. A lot of other experiences I have had with her were very dark and disturbing, but ultimately it helped me achieve something. She often comes across as very intimidating and insensitive. Hela imposes the fact that decay is very important to life. Without decay, nothing can live. This is why it's important to deal with our own emotional issues. What we don't deal with and lay to rest can often fester and become an infection. Anything that is associated with death and decay are good to offer to her. You might try compost heaps, growing roses, cleaning out the dead wood, giving her your sadness, or having skulls of dead creatures around. I once gave her a skeleton key necklace that I put on her statue. She's keeper of secrets and can open any inner or outer doors. It can happen for the good, or for the worse. The bad experiences people have with Hela are a means to an end. In the end, everything turns out the way it's supposed to be. You become ever more changed when working with her. She isn't just a goddess that is associated with death, but also rebirth. What she has to teach are powerful lessons. They aren't fun or amazing experiences, but they are to provide us with something we need in life.

Prayers to Hela

"I call to Hela, Goddess of death and rebirth. I thank you Hela, for helping me to work with the dead. For helping me to realize that decay is important in life. Hail to you Hela, Goddess of Death!"

"Hela, help me to commune with the dead. Help me understand your ways of decay and rot. I wish to work with my ancestors. Please guide me in this endeavor. Help to change my life for the better, allow me to see what needs to be changed and understand how to change it. Hail to you Hela, Goddess of Death!"

Chapter 17

Eir

I met Eir when I wanted to learn some form of healing. It really started when clients started coming to me with certain requests. I had only a small amount of previous experience with healing. I didn't want to start offering a service to people that I didn't have a lot of experience in. I began to dive into Seidr with Eir through prayers. I was nervous because I would typically wait to buy a statue before honoring a deity. I decided that I didn't need a statue to honor or work with her. I used other methods. Typically statues are a way that I use to focus on specific deities. This experience was completely different than the others.

While some of the gods I work with do involve physical labor of some kind, many of them also involve spiritual discipline. Eir was different because she involved both at the same time. If I had to heal someone, I would need to "see" the internal things, or at least have a visual of what I am doing spiritually. She helped me understand things clearly, gave me a few practice runs with people. This particular type of work definitely opened my eyes to what is possible. I started to realize at this point that what I was doing in Seidr, was actually having a real affect on the people I was trying to help. It all became real to me after a while and I stopped questioning if it was just me. The way people were thanking me, the way people were telling me how much better they felt. It all made me realize that this is a serious practice.

My work with Eir didn't just stop at healing. She said that my physical body was very important to helping others. If I couldn't maintain a healthy lifestyle, then I had no business trying to work in healing. She really got me motivated about losing weight. With the help of a friend, I discovered that I could easily lose weight by sticking to a strict calorie diet. It involved eating certain types of foods and limiting the amount of food I was consuming. Eir would often come off to me like a professional doctor. She would urge me to not only lose weight, but exercise. After months of trying to find the right method, I was on the track to losing weight and starting a new way of life. Losing weight was not only just a physical thing for me. It became a religious and spiritual practice that I had to abide by.

I was taught that being overweight is okay, but when my mom had to go to the hospital for her heart, that's when things really started to change for me. I realized that what we eat and how much we consume has everything to do with what happens to us. It doesn't mean that we will be immune to any problems, but it does mean that we will have a less chance of having those problems if we decide to live a healthy lifestyle. I used to weigh two hundred and thirty pounds. My goal was to get to one fifty pounds. I knew if I pushed myself, I could reach that goal, and I knew Eir could help me do that! She provided me with the motivation to get things done. I also saw the damage overeating can do because of the issues my mom was having. In the end, she said if I wanted to be a healer and learn from her, I had to change my life. She said she would help me change it, but I had to work at it with real effort. It wasn't something I took lightly. I knew all to well in the past that the gods could definitely influence my life. At the same time, it wasn't like I didn't want to lose weight. I just wasn't sure how to do it until everything began to fall into place.

What does any of this have to do with Eir? She's a goddess who is widely associated with different forms of healing, physical or otherwise. Of course she would be interested in the well-being of her followers. She has the ability to injure as well as heal with her vast knowledge of herbs, energy work, and wits. She came off to me as a very stern woman, but also very understanding and compassionate. I started to associate her with gold and yellow colors. I would make yellow candles for her and offer her cinnamon apple scents. She seemed to really enjoy those. Eir is like a teacher to me, yet at the same time she's like a colleague. She seems to enjoy helping people. She was totally opposed to the idea of me offering her any blood. She told me that it goes against everything she has worked to achieve. Instead, she just liked the devotion and various things I would offer her. She isn't to incredibly picky. I feel like she enjoys the simple things in life and likes to see people happy and smiling. She'll help anyone who is willing to help themselves, sometimes for a price. In the end, It isn't about just healing the body and soul. Eir teaches how one can transform oneself through metamorphosis. She allows you to dive deep into yourself to find your hidden potential. She takes that, molds it, and helps you create something for yourself. Through the power of body and spirit, she can help heal even the deepest of wounds. She'll stretch your limits if you let her, and she'll show you what you are truly capable of. She doesn't just give you the ability to heal yourself, but the determination to get yourself back on track. If you're finding yourself lacking in body or spirit, call to her, see if she has any wisdom on the matter. Talk to her about your situation, maybe she can point you in the right direction for a better path.

Prayer to Eir

"I call to Eir, Goddess of Healing. Help me to become healthy within mind, body, and soul. Teach me your ways of healing and guide me towards a better life."

Book recommendations

Norse Myths *by Kevin Crossley Holland-* Not the best of retelling the old stories, but it is one of the few out there with a clear understanding of older lore. It's a book that will allow you read it easier. It has some offensive things, but it has a retelling that makes it easy to understand it's the best we have at this given time.

The Prose & Poetic Eddas- You should pick up a copy of one of these English translated books. Buy one or more than one copy. I would recommend that you buy more than one copy over time to see the differences between the translation. Either way, it's a personal choice.

Exploring The Northern Tradition *by Galina Krasskova-* Has good basic information on heathenry that I started out with.

Essential Asatru *by Diana Paxon-* Another basic book for beginners.

Teutonic Magic *by Kveldulf Gundarsson-* Has extensive information about the magic used in Norse Paganism. Most of it concerns the runes. Some of his practices are very restrictive but well worth the read for his insight about the runes.

Northern Tradition for the Solitary Practitioner *by Galina Krasskova-* This book provided me with some interesting ways of prayer towards the Norse gods and goddesses and allowed me to come up with my own way of praying and calling to them on a regular basis, making me feel more connected to them.

Our Troth Volumes 1 & 2 by The Troth Organization- These two books really read as one singular book and provide extensive information of not only religious beliefs, but historical findings and all manner of information pertaining to Norse Paganism. It is highly recommended and a crown jewel in my collection. It is worth the money of buying the two books for the information they contain if you can afford them.

Taking Up the Runes by Diana Paxon- While this book doesn't contain all the information it should or touch on things they chose to leave out, it's still a good book for researching the runes and highly recommended.

Seidr: The Gate is Open *by Katie Gerrard-* This book had some interesting ideas and historical facts in it that helped me understand a basis of Seidr practices.

The Book of Seidr *by Runic John-* The Book of Seidr is a fascinating book. Anyone who is serious about working Seidr or is curious to what it entails should read this book. There are only a handful of books out there on Seidr and this book has put a lot of things into perspective for me in understanding what it is and what it entails.

The Tradition of Household Spirits *by Claude Lecouteux-* The basis of the book is all about the traditions and practices of spirits of the house. It talks about different methods of how to handle spirits but also what some of them are like in behavior and what a few look like. The author covers everything in a historical context.

Visions of Vanaheim *by Nornoriel Lokason-* This book

is the authors experiences with the tribes of Vanaheim. It goes into details about their way of life, where they come from, and what they can help us with in magical pursuits. It's a well thought out book that doesn't impose the authors ideals of their UPG upon you, but instead offers a starting point to work with the Vanir.

Books by Raven Kaldera- While Raven has a bad reputation with most people of Norse Paganism, I do find a lot of his works to be interesting and insightful. However, there is a lot of issues regarding his authority over spirits and gods and how his practices are so restrictive that his books read off as if he's a high and mighty shaman king. Keep in mind that while I recommend his books, there are some problems with them. A lot of these problems pertain to his attitude that you can't change the way the practice is because the spirits told him so or the gods told him so. I am under the impression that the gods and spirits come to us in ways that are different for every person. What is right for him isn't right for others if the spirits tell us to do things differently. Just keep in mind that his work and some of Galina's work is very restrictive and they like to say that their way is the only way from what I have seen. Understand that it isn't, but that this attitude should not make you shy away from these books because there are still some if not a lot of good information within them! A lot of his books list things that are of his own experiences and is not normally within the lore even though some of the lore is covered. For anyone who wants to read his books despite all of this, then go right ahead as I did. These books are as Follows:

The Jotunbok- Filled with interesting stories and rituals

147

towards the Jotunar of the various nine worlds. It has some interesting UPG (Unverified Personal Gnosis) of various Jotunar. Some are well known and others are less known. Either way, it's from their perspective and experience.

Pathwalkers Guide to the Nine Worlds- An interesting book about the Nine Worlds of Yggdrasil and what and who resides within them. There are some exercises within this book that I have used and a lot of what they say in this book is a basic description of what the worlds look like and who inhabits them. There is a lot of UPG in this book.

Wyrdwalkers- A book about various practices concerning what they would term as Northern Tradition Shamanism. It's supposed to be an advanced book for spirit workers. It also ties in to the next book.

Wightridden- A book about possession and working with the spirits of the land, commonly known as wights. This is also an advanced book under their term of Northern Tradition Shamanism. There are some repeats within this book and the book above.

Neolithic Shamanism- This book was actually written by both Raven and Galina. It doesn't really touch base at all with any of the Norse gods and goddesses, but focuses more on practices involving arts and crafts, communication with the elemental spirits of fire, water, air, and earth, plus plant and animal spirits. They offer exercises for each section in a chapter. It's supposed to be used to get more in touch with your local area. It's a really interesting book and is meant for more of a beginner.

Talking to the Spirits- The book teaches you the basics about spirit working and even how to communicate with other people about the differences in their personal gnosis and how to speak to people respectfully without disregarding the other persons differences. This book also talks about how one can develop a better relationship with spirits and using divinitory methods to commune and clarify personal messages that were received by the divine. It also talks about delusions and being delusional, which they explain are different from one another.

Overall, this an effective guide to spirit working that can provide you with creating your own way of practice with spirits and gods but also allow you to obtain an understanding about other people who practice it as well. While this book has only two authors, there are many opinions from other pagans around the world listed in the book which provides you not with just the author's perception, but also that of many other people. Anyone beginning in spirit working or even those who have been for a while, it's a great book to have on your shelf in my opinion!

Drawing Down the Spirits- It's written both by Raven Kaldera and Kenaz Filan. The book is about spirit working, spirit and deity possession in particular. It's very informative and has a lot of good ideas and different methods of practice involved within. However, this book was not intended to be a guide to god or spirit possession. They constantly stress about how possession is not something one should go looking to do because of the dangers and issues involved, which I tend to agree upon. This book is not meant to tell you how to perform possession rites, it is meant for an individual who is already experiencing it.

Needless to say, I feel this book was very informative for what it was. It's filled with loads of experiences from other people on the subject, dealing with dangers, issues, and other things, like community acceptance and how to tell the difference between a fraud and a real possession. All and all, it's quite an interesting book.

Books on Animal & Plant Spirits

I don't know to many books on plant spirits, but when it comes to animals, I look to a particular author that I always find insightful. Lupa is a widely known author for animal spirits that works with them and sells them on her etsy shop. Her books are:

New Paths to Animal Totems-A beginners book on animal spirits

Plant and Fungus Totems-Another beginner book about animal and fungus spirits, similar to the first but still worth buying for the differences.

Fang and Fur Blood and Bone-Lupa's first book really spoke to me. It had interesting ideas ranging from how to connect to animal spirits, how to make your own animal protector, and various other things which I thought were interesting perceptions and ideas.

DIY: Totemism-As you would expect from the title, it is a book about how to communicate with animal spirits in your own way, developing your own style and technique by giving you different ideas of the authors practices and various other practices.

Skin Spirits-An interesting book about animal skins and how you can communicate with them and work with them, providing interesting sources of how to work with skins on a physical level in craft and how to commune with them spiritually.

Books on Crystals, Gems, and Stones

My favorite author on this subject is Judy Hall and her Crystal Bibles. They are informative, talking about various properties of crystals, gems, and stones.

Other books of Interest About Magic and Spirituality

Spiritual Protection By Sophie Reicher- It's filled with exercises concerning spiritual and magical abilities and is essential to a magical or spiritual practice. It involves exercises for grounding, shielding, centering, various methods of cleansing, and explains why they are all needed. It's a very good book, a little odd at some points but definitely opened my eyes to what I needed in my practice.

- **Final thoughts**

This is just my personal list and some of what I have in my own home library. I feel that they have served me well in understanding things thus far in my religion and spirituality and I hope that they will do the same for you.

This book has been my dedication to the gods I work with. It represents my respect and honor towards them. May it help you do the same.

Author information:

ravenousnightwind@gmail.com

ravenousnightwind.tumblr.com

Printed in Great Britain
by Amazon.co.uk, Ltd.,
Marston Gate.